"In *Surviving the Wild*, Kimberly Anne steps out of the Midwest and into a life that refuses to stay predictable. This compact memoir follows her through Belize, Panama, and Costa Rica as she rides a roller coaster of reinvention, sometimes stepping into danger and then learning to read the signs that it is time to change course again. She is unlearning the cultural training that teaches women to ignore their instincts. She offers the reader the electric recognition that this author is telling the messy truth. Kimberly reveals a woman rebuilding her inner compass while shaping a life that feels real, spacious, and deeply lived. *Surviving the Wild* is a countercultural invitation to anyone who feels that tug toward a life not yet named. Her journey exemplifies the courage it takes to leave what is familiar and reach for something truer."

– Amy Lou Jenkins, award-winning author of Every Natural Fact

"*Surviving the Wild* resonates powerfully with Thoreau's adage that most people are living lives of quiet desperation. Kimberly Anne's story recounts her sometimes joyful and often painful journey of escape. Beyond the gravitas, there is also much good humor. The question for her readers is 'Red Pill? Or Blue?'"

– Max Oelschlaeger, author of The Idea of Wilderness

"The tribe of wild women is one that has existed since the beginning of time. Although rarely acknowledged publicly, every woman has the opportunity to be initiated. The call to face the inner voice is a powerful one, and the courage required to explore it is remarkable. In her stark authenticity and vulnerability, Kimberly Anne pulls back the curtain and gives a peek at the pivotal moments of transformation where both choices and courage can lead a woman into a level of wild freedom that exists beyond the confines of societal limitations. In diving into Kimberly Anne's story, we all get to be part of the tribe as we are transported through her reflections of past, present, and future potential wildness. If your inner voice calls you to feel wild, if you ever feel alone, or if you're seeking the courage to listen to your inner voice, Kimberly Anne and her stories will inspire you on your way."

– Dove Crawford, M.S., advanced registered yoga teacher

SURVIVING the WILD

SURVIVING
the WILD

AN UNTAMED WOMAN
OPENS HER CAGE

AWAKEN ◆ VILLAGE
—— PRESS ——

Copyright © 2026 by Kimberly Anne
All rights reserved.

Editing by Grace Adamarie Watson
Cover and interior design by Andrea Gibb
Author photo by Daniel Rivas Photography Studio

ISBN 978-1-957408-27-9 (paperback)
ISBN 978-1-957408-28-6 (ebook)

Library of Congress Control Number: 2025924906

Published by Awaken Village Press, Sioux Falls, SD
www.awakenvillagepress.com

To the ones who held me while I unraveled and rewrote. And to all the creatures I've crossed paths with—thank you for showing me love in your way.

"WILD WOMEN ARE AN
UNEXPLAINABLE SPARK OF LIFE.
THEY OOZE FREEDOM AND SEEK
AWARENESS, THEY BELONG TO
NOBODY BUT THEMSELVES YET
GIVE A PIECE OF WHO THEY ARE
TO EVERYONE THEY MEET.

IF YOU HAVE MET ONE, HOLD ON
TO HER, SHE'LL ALLOW YOU INTO
HER CHAOS BUT SHE'LL ALSO
SHOW YOU HER MAGIC."

— *Nikki Rowe*

dear wild ones

In 2014, I was milking goats on my hobby farm in Wisconsin, blissfully unaware that ten years later I'd be divorced, have fallen wildly in and out of love four or five times, and be living on a tiny island in Central America with a man I'd spent five minutes with. If someone had predicted that, I'd have assumed they were tripping or nipping on something strong. But here we are—in 2025—and every bit of it happened.

Then, another impulsive move to the jungle cracked open a whole new life, one that eventually led me to another Caribbean island and to a version of myself I hadn't yet met. This book is my messy, magical, deeply personal take on what happens when you stop living the life you were told to want and start chasing the one that sets your soul on fire.

I've lived Carlos Castaneda's words: "For me there is only the traveling on paths that have heart ...." Let me tell you: following a path with heart is not for the faint of spirit. It demands courage, curiosity, and a willingness to leap before you look. But the journey—oh, the journey—is everything.

In the past two years alone, I've lived, loved, and learned more than in any other chapter of my life—and I already had a pretty remarkable life. My time abroad has changed me. From the earth to the sky and everything in between, I see it all differently now.

This book is for me. But more importantly, this book is for you, for the person who dreams—has always dreamed—of another path in life. This book is a love letter to those dreamers, especially women, who feel that tug toward something more. It's a challenge to break free from the grind, the expectations, the soul-sucking routines we've been sold as "success." Western culture has us overworked, overstressed, and under-inspired. But what if joy—ecstatic, unfiltered joy—is still possible? With or without a man. With or without stuff. With just you, your heart, and the wild unknown.

Surviving the Wild is for anyone who's ever whispered, "What if?" and dared to listen to what comes next. It's a call to be brave, to be scared, and to go ahead anyway. Because the life you're meant for isn't in your comfort zone—it's out there, in the wild, waiting for you to show up.

"TO TRAVEL IS WORTH ANY COST
OR SACRIFICE."

– Elizabeth Gilbert

chapter one

THE ISLAND OF
UNFINISHED BUSINESS

Rolling over in bed on the morning of November 13, 2023, still hovering between dreamland and consciousness at 2:45 a.m., I mindlessly looked at my phone and was suddenly jolted awake. All cylinders were firing up, the wheels in my head turning as rapidly as they could at this ungodly hour. I needed to process the situation quickly. What the fuck was happening? Was what I was seeing on my phone real? Why did I suddenly feel like Jennifer Lopez in every action movie where she has amazing arm muscles and needs to fight off some crazy ex-lover? I realized I had to escape this island—not only the island but the country—immediately.

I knew I had less than five days to escape. It's not that I was breaking any laws—my passport had just been stamped in Panama, so I wasn't due to pay the fee for the thirty-day visitor's permit again in Belize until December. I had only been living on the little island for three months. When you're used to living in large cities in the U.S., trying to figure out how to live in a third-world country in Central America—on a tiny island of 1,000 people, no less—is as hard as it sounds. But so much had already happened in my short amount of time there. I had started to make friends, build community, and establish a routine, which was no easy feat. I had lived landlocked for my entire life, with no ocean for hundreds—usually thousands—of miles.

Growing up in the Midwest, I was surrounded by small (minuscule, really) bodies of water, but I had only been on an island once before (Alcatraz doesn't count). In 2014, my then-husband and I went with his SCUBA diving group to a very small island in Fiji for ten days. I was lucky enough to bring two special girlfriends with me, one of whom also had her SCUBA certification and spent most of the time touring, island-hopping, and getting to know the local people and their culture with the two of us.

None of us had met happier people than the Fijians. In terms of material belongings, they don't have much at all, but they exude joy and community, even taking care of each other's children. Sometimes I would see very small kids playing near the ocean or seemingly unattended, and when I asked someone about it, they would casually explain that there was nothing to worry about—someone was always watching. They even fed and disciplined neighborhood children regardless of whether they belonged to their family. It wasn't only acceptable; it was expected. It was an unspoken rule. It was community.

I would learn this type of Fijian joy and unlimited happiness for myself ten years later in Costa Rica, but first I had to get safely off that island in Belize. After the initial shock to my nervous system decreased enough that I could stop shaking, I realized plans had to be set in motion immediately. But it was the middle of the night. I couldn't turn any lights on, wanting to appear that I wasn't awake or even at home. I didn't want him to know where I was. I had to wait for daylight. The only thing I could do was try to remain calm and get a little more sleep, if I could even do that.

It seems a little dramatic, not being allowed to turn the lights on in my own apartment. But I had my rationale, and I knew I had to trust my gut instinct. It was what had—and always would—keep me alive. I've made several missteps in life, as we all have, and I'd say about seventy-five percent of those missteps were when I ignored my intuition. This usually occurred when I really wanted to do something, and then I would reconcile the aftermath later, acknowledging what I indeed knew deep down would inevitably happen. That intuitive gut feeling was now telling me I needed to be off the island before 6 p.m. on Saturday, in just five days. Quick decisions would have to be made with minimal but critical information. I had just returned from two weeks of traveling through Costa Rica and northern Panama, and while I planned to return to Costa Rica in December, after it had captivated me so much, now my flight would need to be moved forward to November 18th.

This new information made me wonder about my near future and the quality of life on that island. It was a case of "want" versus "don't want." What did I want? To feel safe. What didn't I want? To die. Was there a higher probability than usual that the latter could occur? I must have been pretty convinced there was, or I wouldn't be fleeing a country to be out of the reach of one man.

One Tuesday morning eight months prior, I was knee-deep in tight deadlines and called my friend Mia. The moment I told her, "I am not okay," she knew something was wrong, very different than usual. I was catastrophically burnt out from my corporate America job as well as the nonsense and fuckery that came with the recent years of romantic entanglements I had allowed myself to be ensnared in. I had been divorced for ten years, but I had hit the dating scene right after that, much sooner than I maybe should have. Whether you want to call it "dating" or "humping," I had gotten back on that proverbial horse quickly after my fourteen-year marriage came to an end. Physically, emotionally, spiritually, I was at a breaking point I hadn't experienced in quite a while, if ever before. I was ready to wave the white flag and tap out.

Almost immediately after my divorce, I fell in love—hard. It was the kind of love you don't recover from, the kind that changes your perspective of the world. The experience felt like running full speed down a concrete sidewalk, tripping and falling on your face, teeth chipped and broken, just like your heart. But it wasn't meant to turn into any kind of stable relationship at that time. Five months after that, I met a wonderful guy, and we almost made it to the five-year mark of our relationship. I felt the "ghost" of the previous man, the imprint of his heart (and soul) on me, the entire time though. Four months after the five-year relationship ended, the "ghost" re-entered my life and said, "It's time for us." When that ended, I tried to stifle the pain by jumping into a few new beds (with very hot men in them) and one very short but very passionate and incredibly destructive relationship. I was exhausted.

Mia and I had met in high school. By the age of seventeen, we were both independent of our nuclear families and raising ourselves. Ever since, we'd always known we had each other. As we talked on the phone that day, Mia confessed that she was at a very similar breaking point and also needed to get away. I had been randomly searching Caribbean vacation spots, and prices had dictated that I get creative. Belize was a country that had always been in the back of my mind for some reason, and it happened to be friendly in terms of both climate and budget. I was planning on meditating, doing yoga, and sitting in the sand on the beach with a bottle of tequila—or rum—we'd be in the Caribbean, after all. Mia said she was in, and I began to find a place for us to escape to for temporary reunion and relief.

Eight days later, my best friend of thirty years and I would be flying into Dallas from different states and then jumping on a flight together to head to Belize. As I prepared for the travel day, I was tired, heartbroken, and ungrounded. I had allowed people and circumstances to take things from my spirit that I knew were rightfully mine. Me at full strength would never have allowed it, but this version of me had been worn down by years of immense, intense love, pain, joy, sorrow, and dating. In some ways, the two years prior had been the best, as I had started to travel more and gotten to experience wickedly passionate love affairs that all came with heartbreak on some level. They were also the hardest on me emotionally and mentally. I was pushed to my limits in every way, including physically, as I had to overcome two winter illnesses plus a bout with COVID, which had finally caught me in 2022.

One of those anxious fliers, I left at 3:30 a.m. for my 6:00 a.m. flight. I hated feeling rushed. I also hated to fly and got severely motion sick, so I had been pre-medicating for forty-eight hours already. Knowing we were going to be in the air and on water, I wanted to be sure this very short vacation would be enjoyed to its fullest. Neither of us had been to Central America before, and getting from the mainland to the little island we were staying on required some advance planning. Most of all, I was nervous about making my connecting flight in Dallas. I had the shortest layover at the fourth-busiest U.S. airport, just thirty-nine minutes to navigate DFW, which was also big as fuck. High risk, high reward.

It had been a year and three months since Mia and I had

seen each other and vowed then not to let more than a year go by between visits. Before that, it had been at least five years. She was my original "ride or die" before that was even a phrase. There weren't even camera phones when we pulled the wild and crazy shit we used to—thank goodness! I was ready to jump out of my seat and kick heads out of the way so I could run through the airport terminals and be reunited with my girl.

As soon as that plane came to a stop in Dallas, I stood up, unclipped my seatbelt, and threw my backpack on. (Yup, this time I would be one of "those" airplane people.) My suitcase was already checked through to Belize, so I scurried off the plane and jumped onto the airport train for the international terminal. As I rushed through the airport, my phone pinged every few seconds with Mia's updates on what was going on at the boarding gate. Two nights beforehand, when I told her I had been concerned about making my connection, she stopped me mid-sentence and said, "Hey, do you really think I'm going to let that plane take off without you? You know I'm not letting that pilot go anywhere until I'm with you!" We both laughed, knowing it was true, and it did a lot to curb my connecting flight anxiety.

I still wanted to move quickly, but I knew Mia would do anything to keep me safe and make sure I made it to that plane. Given how important travel and freedom are to both of us, I knew she wouldn't risk losing her passport by tying the pilot up with her Gucci scarf, but Mia is extremely persuasive and as brilliant as she is stunningly beautiful. All she'd really have to do would be to bend over (or just stand—who are we kidding?) in the aisle near the cockpit, and the pilot would temporarily forget his schedule. That pilot didn't stand a chance!

I texted her when I got on the train, then again when I got

to our terminal, and even at the boarding gate. When I finally saw her in the first row (of course, my luxurious friend flies first class), I burst into tears, falling into her arms for a moment before laughing and saying I needed to go to the back of the aircraft with the "poor people." Everyone up in first class laughed along with me as I walked away on that note.

We had both made it. My solo trip for healing and working on my shit had turned into something much more: a reunion with my most cherished friend. Somehow, Mia and I had never taken a trip together before, and we vowed we would never wait until we're both in crisis mode to take one ever again.

The first night we arrived, thanks to some duty-free mezcal and vodka, we had our very own dance party at our boutique resort's poolside bar. We were the only two people outside and wildly dancing around, at that. I can only imagine what the bartender was thinking: "I only gave them pineapple juice, why are they so lit?" Well, I had been going back to our room every once in a while to top our juice off with liquor.

In truth, we were so happy and at peace to be in this tropical paradise with each other that we would have been dancing, buzzed or not. Mia and I do what we want, which is a sentiment that's heightened tenfold when we're together. Each of us had gotten so used to working hard from a young age, fighting our way through life (each in different ways) to thrive and survive. What resulted was a lack of the shy self-consciousness that other women often seemed to struggle with. We didn't need any liquid courage to be ourselves; we would just stop, drop, and dance. Now at a new age and stage—both divorced and in our late forties—we were two brave spirits, independent, adventurous, and comfortable in our own skin. We had been through so much and no longer used verbal filters to express ourselves.

Strong bitches like us are as real as it gets. They're also the most dangerous kind of woman: the untamed kind.

Mia is a tall, dark, gorgeous Native American woman. I am almost her photo negative: pale, blonde, and tiny but mighty. As Shakespeare once said, "Though she be but little, she is fierce." That's me in a nutshell: a pitbull attitude in a chihuahua body. My nervous system doesn't know "flight" or "freeze;" it only knows "fight," an ironic outcome for an overprotected child whose default was to be afraid of everything. I may not win a fight, but I'll always rally and try to overcome the danger or obstacle.

Mia and I were opposite in physical appearance but identical in Amazonian woman spirit. Belizean men were always tripping over their tongues, staring at her. No one even noticed she was walking with anyone as they asked if they could do anything for her, pointing her in the right direction or just catcalling. The funny thing is, she never noticed them, and neither ,of us cared. We were just so happy to be together and away from reality for a few days. I'd like to insert here that we had agreed this trip wouldn't be about dick. We would not be on a manhunt!

Time moved slowly there. Even though we had packed a lot of sightseeing in, it never felt like we were rushed as we moved around the island by bike or golf cart, as no other vehicles were allowed. We rode the dirt streets in search of serene stretches of beach, charming restaurants, and friendly strangers. The beautiful Belizean people represent a true melting pot of cultures. Those who are native to the country look like they are from Latin America or even Africa. Of the amazingly diverse population, the large settlement of Mennonites in the north-central part of the country, whose appearance reflects their European ancestors, is the only demographic I might be able to blend in with. They have not mixed with other Belizeans and are still fair-skinned with light eyes and lighter hair. But my shorter hair, large tattoos, and summer shorts sized for a third-grader would immediately give away that I was likely never part of that community.

Though the country's official language is English, most people seemed to default to their native tongue of Belizean Kriol, a form of Creole. When they spoke English, they did so with a very Caribbean accent that was both beautiful and sexy. Sprinkled in alongside these languages were also Spanish as well as some indigenous languages.

We met a lot of local people, each with their own story of how they ended up on this small island. Many had come from the mainland but never traveled outside of Belize, as it is difficult and expensive to get a passport there. While having coffee in San Pedro on a neighboring island one day, we struck up a conversation with a local Belizean man who had traveled extensively throughout the U.S. After telling him I lived in Tucson, Arizona, he said he really enjoyed a restaurant there named Li'l Abner's Steakhouse. It is actually a well-known dinner spot, recognized for its steaks and rustic cowboy atmosphere. How incredibly random that a Central American man, a world away, knew the name of this locally owned restaurant!

That man and I had switched places temporarily: he visited my homeland, and I was now visiting his. It was only two people taking vacations, yes, but now we were tied to each other, cosmically speaking. We shared the big blue marble of Earth, and now we had seen a little bit of each other's place on it. This complete stranger had seen into part of my world and culture, and I his and nothing and no one would take that experience or that common bond away.

As we travel and experience other people and cultures, whether 100 miles or 5,000 from where we started, we become open to new and different people, environments that teach us not only about others but also so incredibly much about ourselves. The difference in how we approach life, each other, and even some of our views are changed—hopefully for the better—once our eyes have been opened to new things. I know mine did. After all, that's what it's all about. If we're lucky enough to be in the position to travel and explore the world, which in turn allows us to explore ourselves more deeply, we should seize that opportunity. What a gift. Our frames of reference broaden as the proverbial lens that we see the world through changes. We grow. Grow, baby, grow.

Mia and I made the absolute most of our five days in that tropical climate of our little island and others, hopping around when we wanted to go on excursions. That Saturday in San Pedro and the island of Ambergris Caye, we spent the afternoon at a place called Secret Beach before returning to our little island of Caye Caulker to enjoy one final night together. While we waited for the water taxi that would take us from the main village to our resort for the last time, we took some pictures of the ocean, the brightly colored buildings, and anything else we thought was picture-worthy. Some fellow tourists gave us a hand as we posed for one more photo. Then, walking to the end of the pier and turning toward the ocean, we each placed one arm around the other and gazed out at the sea. With Mia holding tightly to my waist, I couldn't remember the last time I had felt so safe or at peace. I could feel her power and stillness, admiring both of us. Life had added up and weighed us down, but we still had the strength to keep each other afloat.

The next morning, we took our last water taxi to the main village and came across a sweet outdoor cafe on the way to the airport. Surrounded by lush plants, we had a great last breakfast at Wheezie's before checking in for our flight from Caye Caulker to the international airport on the mainland in Belize City.

Waiting for our flight, we captured a few more photos and videos of the tropical surroundings of the tiny airport. I turned to look down the runway, and leaning up against the side of a long building stood one of the most beautiful, unique-looking men I'd ever seen in person. He looked like a Rastafarian, with hair well past his knees in thick dreadlocks braided together. He was so striking, with smooth dark skin, extremely high cheekbones, and almost black eyes that had a faraway look in them. I told Mia I really wanted a photo with this man, one of the airport employees, but I was embarrassed to ask. He didn't look like the kind of guy who'd want to pose for a photograph, but I talked myself into asking anyway. He was so visually stunning that I thought, *Fuck it. When would I ever see this guy again?* Completing my trip photos with an image of this intriguing character just needed to happen.

As I got closer to the man, his energy felt grounded and quiet yet strong. His expression didn't change much as I approached him, but I wished I knew what he was thinking behind those eyes that held so much emotion. I detected all this "stuff" in his eyes—wisdom, experience, memories, happy moments, and very bad ones. He agreed to let me take a picture with him, and I barely got a smile out of him. I cautiously put my hand on his back and got close for the picture. Thanking him and saying goodbye, I walked off to be with Mia and wait for our tiny island plane.

Once through security at Belize City's airport, we started getting notifications on our phones that the Belize to Dallas flight was further and further delayed. Thirty minutes after making our way through customs, it was clear I would never make my second flight from Dallas home to Tucson. Looking at Mia, I said, "I'd rather be in Belize one more day than stuck in a hotel in Dallas for twenty-four hours."

Staying would require telling my new boss I wouldn't be at work the following day and checking if one of my pet sitters could take care of Pesto, my cat, for a little longer. Then I would have to figure out how to get back to the island. I wanted to exit the airport to see what my transportation options would be from there (whether small charter plane or water taxi), but the same customs clerk who had looked at my passport said that once I stepped outside the airport doors, I would need to go through customs all over again. It was a wildly spontaneous idea, a hassle that could very well be an unsafe bet, and all while practically boarding a flight. Feeling a little defeated, I turned around and told Mia I should just go to Dallas. It seemed like the sanest, most logical option, even if that's not usually my style.

In spite of my hesitation, Mia encouraged me to stay, but I was afraid to do so without her. She's always been so protective of me, and I knew she would do anything to make sure I was never harmed. Was it too crazy, though, to try to fend for myself in Belize? I knew I wouldn't stay on the mainland and would have to get back to our island, where I felt safer and had met a few people in our short time there. "You need to stay," she stated firmly. As she did, I could feel that it was the option the Universe wanted me to choose, and Mia knew it too.

The friendly and accommodating manager at the airline counter rebooked my tickets to travel the exact same times and flights, but on Monday instead of Sunday. The expense of another day of travel (and pet sitting) wasn't something I needed at the time, but I was excited about the challenge and the gift of one more night in that place. Nervous, I shed a couple of tears as I said goodbye to Mia, who needed to catch our original flight to Dallas. She hugged me tight, handed me a fistful of cash, told me she loved me, and said, "Go back. You're supposed to." She walked away, and I turned the other direction, a tear running down my cheek as I passed through those airport doors I had been forbidden to walk out of moments earlier. I had no idea just how much that extra day in Belize would change the trajectory of my life.

"WE TRAVEL, SOME OF US
FOREVER, TO SEEK OTHER
STATES, OTHER LIVES, OTHER
SOULS."

— anaïs nin

chapter two

BELIZE IS MISSING YOU TOO

Starting my journey back to Caye Caulker, I hired a ground taxi to take me to the ferry drop-off. My driver, Lionel, was just the best—a retired first responder and volunteer fireman who was also on the city council and played several other roles in service to his community, such as taxi driving. I purchased a ticket and then waited for a short time before boarding the boat back.

Once I arrived back on the tiny island, I stopped at the nearest bar, plugged in my nearly dead phone, and booked a night at a little hotel with small cabanas, perfect for one person. After enjoying a conch steak dinner, I hopped on a water taxi to return to the resort Mia and I had stayed at, excited to spend the evening hanging with our new friends—the bartenders. They were surprised to see me again as I sat down at the bar and explained what happened.

That night, a very hot and very young twenty-two-year-old bartender (so young looking I asked to see his driver's license, so I knew he was legal!) escorted me back to my hotel room. With the entire island's dim street lights, everything looked so unfamiliar at night, so I was grateful for the company. He came inside, and things got flirty. I mean, if you consider taking your top off "flirty." But how else are you going to show your tattoos when they are requested to be seen?

We started kissing, but he confessed he couldn't stay very long, and I thought, *Why? Do you have school in the morning, kiddo? Yikes.* I asked if he had someone waiting at home, and he said he did, so I promptly thanked him for walking me to my hotel and for fondling my boobs and then kicked him out. Bonus: he forgot the dinner the fancy resort kitchen had sent him home with, and I ate the entire thing. I felt I earned my feline stripes that night. Good times.

As I ate, I thought about what a bizarre situation that was and smiled about how often weird, fun shit happens to me. That guy was so beautiful, and all night I couldn't figure out why he was staring at me so strangely. Every time he walked toward my side of the bar, he'd stare—longer than what was the social norm. I figured it was because I was a foreigner and looked different, but I knew this high-end boutique hotel hosted people from all over the world. Surely he was used to seeing blonde hair and blue eyes.

It took me a while to get it, but when we finally started talking, I realized he was seriously attracted to me. This wasn't the first time a hot young guy had shown interest in me, but I hadn't been interpreting this one's signals correctly. I never would have guessed that he was gazing at me for so long because he was eye-fucking me (which means pretty much what it sounds like: someone finds you highly attractive and thinks it would be groovy to see you without pants on). I mean, age aside, I'm still not everyone's cup of tea. I'm no curvy supermodel and not the typical aesthetic men in that part of the world find attractive. Of course, when the eye-fucking is going *both* ways, look out! That kind of connection and chemistry can't be ignored.

I don't typically make the first move because I need a man who's strong enough and confident enough to go after what he wants, even if that's me. Especially if that's me. As I learned from a recent discussion with one of the beautiful men in my life, men prefer to hunt, not to *be* hunted. Where is the handbook where all of these rules and assumptions are kept though? I feel like I've learned everything the hard way: through trial and error. In the end, maybe we're all confused as fuck out here, and we just let our hormone-driven hoo-hahs and ding-a-lings take over.

As I was packing again in the morning, one of my best friends texted to see if I'd had a good time on my bonus day on Caye Caulker. I replied with what was possibly the most succinct text I've ever sent: "Definitely." Reason being, I was doing mental gymnastics again to make sure I'd be able to get from the tiny island back to the mainland and then to (and through) the airport. She immediately texted back with, "That answer is giving me 'I need more details' vibes." Laughing out loud, I dialed her number, as I knew it was expected of me.

I didn't get around that much, but I also didn't mind recalling a fun night when I'd had one, and my friends had gotten the impression that I'd more than earned my cougar status (an older woman and much younger man relationship). I was known for stumbling upon (not hunting) my prey, playing with them for a while before either walking away to find fresh meat or becoming attached to one of them and allowing him to entangle me in a sordid but insanely passionate relationship.

After my phone call, I knew I wanted to eat at the cafe Mia and I had visited the morning before. The island is so small that I had already memorized certain landmarks, and directions were easy to figure out in the daylight, as the pretty water with the reef was on the west, with the darker water to the east. I turned right from the cabana and found the road I knew Wheezie's Cafe was on. I walked by the same buildings we'd seen the day before and smiled at a man walking his very energetic German Shepherd puppy. As they passed, I heard a noise behind me and turned to see bicycle tires. Looking up to see who was riding the bike, my eyes grew wide. It was the gorgeous man I had taken the photo with at the airport, with his long, dark braids and pants at least three sizes too big. He looked like he had come straight out of a Death Row Records music video.

He slowed down and got off his bike to walk with me, steering with one hand and holding a cup of coffee in the other. I smiled big, and he did too. It surprised me; I had the sense from the day before that it wasn't natural for him to be so expressive.

"Hi!" I said, wide-eyed and waving.

He continued grinning. "I recognized you from your tattoo," he said, pointing to my arm. "But what are you doing back here?"

I laughed and explained what had happened when I tried to leave. We chatted for a few moments before he went off to the airport for work, and I continued to the cafe, saying I would see him soon to catch my flight off the little island. I did see him again at the airport, and we exchanged phone numbers when he said it would be cool to have one of the photos I had taken the day before. Once I reached the mainland, I sent him the photos. He thanked me and mentioned he'd keep in touch. Smiling, I put my phone away and boarded my flight to Tucson.

When I landed in Tucson and turned my phone back on that evening, I already had a message from him, from Rasta.

"Kimberly, I wanted to see if you reach home safe yet."

"Wow, that's so sweet of you!" I wrote back. "We just touched down, so I will be home in about thirty minutes. Hope you had a great day. So glad we ran into each other again."

"I'm glad you already touched down I wanted to ask you what is your birth sign if it's okay with you," he responded, his lack of punctuation simultaneously primitive and endearing. It matched the way he spoke English with his Belizean Kriol accent. "And by the way my day went beautiful and it's blessed now that I know you're safe."

Surprised by his question, I told him I was a Capricorn and asked him the same before putting away my phone and heading home from the airport. Now, ladies, a straight man asking for your zodiac sign is like a purple unicorn: it doesn't exist. I mean, compared to the other kinds of texts guys send, it was a pretty thoughtful and wholesome message, right?

Once I was home, I saw his answer: he was a Leo. My jaw dropped. "Another Leo!" I wrote back to him. "Leos are my favorite. There are so many Leos in my life."

What?! Many of my best female friends were also Leos born in July or August, but the fellas I'd fallen hard for were all August-born Leos. Why did the Universe keep dropping these gorgeous, magnetic Leos onto my lap? There are many people out there who think those of us who put faith in the zodiac when choosing romantic partners are crazy "basic bitches" (i.e., astrology following, yoga pants wearing, pumpkin spice latte drinking— but, to clarify, I hate pumpkin spice in my coffee!). Well, this basic bitch had done a little research, and I could confirm that I was drawn to, even unnaturally obsessed with, Leos. It was like I had a full-on collection of them, so much so that if a "sexual serial killer" were a thing, I might have had to turn myself in. Though if anything, they killed me: my heart, specifically. I had turned my life, my heart, and my body inside out for these August Leos. They were a hot, confident, passionate bunch, but all I wanted to do by now was run away from any new ones. They always seemed to leave me limping away afterwards, wondering, *What the fuck just happened?* as I tried to piece my life back together.

I let Rasta know I had made it home safely and was already missing Belize.

"You may be missing Belize," he said, "but believe if you don't know, Belize is missing you too."

If this were a movie, that would be the moment when the female lead drops her pants and lunges for the love interest (okay, maybe she just leans in for a kiss—no need to go from zero to ho right away). I was stunned by the level of emotion I picked up from his message. I'd never heard a more beautiful, poetic, and blatantly honest statement. It was as if Rasta was confessing something that was too pure to be a lie. I told him that it was a beautiful thing to say and that he was good with words.

"I don't think so and don't really like texting but your vibe is blessed with mines," he explained. "You're a very cool person and I would really like to get to know more about you."

Feeling touched and flattered, I told him I believed that the Universe always brought people together for reasons we couldn't always know at first. To me, I explained, there were no accidents.

"I guess the universe has its balance," he texted back. Then, he admitted that a question lingered on his mind. "I know you may not know me but what was your sight when you looked at me for the first time?"

I thought for a moment, recalling how the sight of him struck me when I first saw Rasta at the airport. "Well," I wrote, "I thought you were beautiful to look at, and I liked your energy. I'm very sensitive to energy around me, and I feel it especially when someone is close by."

"You really put a smile on my face," he replied, bringing a smile to my face. "If by chance we should meet again would you think it's possible for us to spend time and see if we are compatible?"

I told him I would like that, genuinely intrigued by this interesting man. With that, we wished each other blessed nights and concluded the conversation.

In all truth, the situation may have been a combination of a little bit of love and infatuation at first sight. The moment I saw Rasta at the airport, and again in the middle of a bumpy dirt road in Belize when I was supposed to be back in the United States, my brain broke. On him, even that baggy airport uniform looked attractive. I fell a little bit in love (or infatuation) when he had already messaged to make sure I'd made it home safe.

You see, I struggle to feel safe, always wishing there was someone other than myself to help protect me. I know I'm responsible for myself, but there's still that part of me that wants a romantic relationship with someone who's strong (but able to express emotions) and protective (but not aggressive), who cares about where I'm at, if I've arrived, and how I'm doing. I'm hoping we can all recognize that these are big feelings to have in response to what is basically the bare minimum of kindness, but Rasta had a calm, grounded energy, along with some swagger, whether or not he was aware of it. I don't want some egotistical pendejo, but I do appreciate a humble confidence—that's a total panty dropper. Literally, a little swagger goes a long way with me.

For two people who may not look like a match on paper, we seemed to have a pretty strong connection for some reason. Rasta came across as a man of few words who was very straightforward and intentional when he spoke, and I was at that age where I didn't mess around. What you saw was what you got, and I was going to tell you all about it, whatever "it" was at any given moment.

On my third day back home in Tucson, we were on a second day of rain, and I was already overwhelmed by the fast-paced Western culture, a big reason I had needed to leave for the island in the first place. The other reason was that I'd had a couple of brief but intense love affairs in the past year, and I hadn't fully worked through them enough to heal my heart. In addition was all the other life stuff that gets thrown at us daily. It had all added up, and I desperately needed to slow down, breathe, and work on these issues. Luckily, I'd heard the warning bell and dropped everything to go to Belize. The trip was about healing and giving my bruised heart a break.

I lead my life with an open heart. I'm strong as fuck, but I'm also willing to be vulnerable for the right adventure, the right love, or the right guy (no matter the length of the relationship). Life is, after all, about experiences. When I feel an energy or connection that transcends the everyday, I wonder if it might become something extraordinary. Those are the chances I take without hesitation—always. So, there I was, sipping my morning coffee in Tucson, Arizona, having a text message conversation with a man on an island in Belize.

"I always said to myself I wasn't going to rush to get back into a relationship but you came along and I really like your vibe," he wrote. "I would love to try something with you. You never know it's always good to have someone on your side ...."

"I agree," I typed back. "I just came off of a year of intense relationships and heartbreak, so I'm not in a hurry either, but you intrigue me. I like your vibe too."

"I think it was meant to be though," he said. "I know we would make a perfect couple. I just feel it ... I feel like I've known you from a long time ago and know when I get to know you it's going to be deeper."

"Yeah, it feels that way to me too."

We continued to learn about each other, discussing our favorite types of alcohol and whether we smoked weed (though it was apparent he did, judging not just by his look but by the marijuana leaf tattoo on his neck). He was distinctive, with his striking appearance, calm demeanor, and way of talking—low and slow (could be the marijuana!) and with the sexiest Caribbean accent. Truthfully, none of the things that drew me to him could give me much of a clue as to who he was as a person, but I was intrigued. Because his beautiful twisted locs (dreadlocks) fell in braids below his knees, I asked if he was a Rastafarian. He said he wasn't; he just hated getting haircuts. It made me laugh to think of all of that gorgeous hair existing for no other reason than an aversion to haircuts.

All of a sudden, it felt as though I might end up in some sort of long-distance situationship. As the weeks passed by, Rasta would receive photos of me dancing, of my cat, and even meals I made. You have to get creative when long-distance dating. It requires lots of calls, messages, photos, and video chats. Because I went out and did a lot of Latin dancing, I asked if Rasta liked to dance. He said he didn't like large crowds and preferred to do his own thing, stay close to home, listen to music, and chill. He seemed introverted for an August-born Leo and said he was terrible at dancing but that I could teach him a few moves.

I sent him a couple of videos of me doing some Latin and African dancing with different partners so he'd get an idea of what I actually did as a hobby. One video was of me and a friend dancing to bachata music, which is a pretty sensual dance, very up close and personal with the other dancer. Rasta's response was to compliment me, rather than giving the stereotypically sexual response many guys might make about my tight outfit. In fact, we'd been talking for a month and he had yet to say anything remotely inappropriate. I'd never met a man like that, who was laid back and a little shy but able to express himself. Once, recounting a naughty cat story, I even described my cat, Pesto, as a "dick," and Rasta said, "Don't talk about your little creature that way." It made me laugh to think about the demanding, furry asshole who thinks of me as his servant, as my "little creature."

I asked Rasta's age since this cougar had been hunting among some young lion prides lately, and was relieved when I learned he was thirty-six and not twenty-six or younger. We talked a little about our jobs, and then he asked if I was planning to come back to Belize any time soon. I said that I would love to, that Belize was good for my soul, and I had already been tracking flights to see when the best time would be to return.

"I'll be here patiently waiting for you," he replied. "Maybe we drink some tequila and watch the sunset together."

It sounded perfect, but, considering my track record, I knew I needed to ask an important question.

"How many kids, wives, or girlfriends do you have? For the record, I have none," I joked.

"None of the above," he wrote back. "Free, single, and disengaged."

He was surprised that I didn't have any kids, and I explained that I'd never wanted any but that I was helping one of my best friends with his seventeen-year-old son, which I loved being able to do. Rasta told me that his aunt had advised him not to rush to have any kids and that he had taken her words seriously. He'd had a girlfriend for three of the six years he had spent on the island, but she "had too many tricks up her sleeves." He didn't like playing games and said he'd rather be single than deal with that.

"That's wise," I answered. "I don't fuck around or play

games. I'm pretty transparent, and I speak the truth—too much, sometimes." I agreed it was way better to be single than to settle for anything less than what you want and deserve. If only I could always obey my own wisdom.

From an emotional standpoint, we seemed to understand and want what the other wanted in a partner. As for our lifestyles, we couldn't be more different. We had some intense and deep conversations about things you normally have to wait weeks or months to discuss in the normal dating scene. We were half a world away from each other, and we had nothing to hide, so we didn't.

The cold desert rain was making me miss Belize that much more. So, just weeks after coming back, I bought a plane ticket to return and stay even longer this time—five months longer.

"THE PURPOSE OF LIFE IS TO
LIVE IT, TO TASTE EXPERIENCE
TO THE UTMOST, TO REACH
OUT EAGERLY AND WITHOUT
FEAR FOR NEWER AND RICHER
EXPERIENCE."

– Eleanor Roosevelt

chapter three

WILD ENOUGH TO LEAVE

For some reason, the Belizean customs agents thought that a small American woman trying to enter their country with four suitcases was a code-red crisis. The long travel day was a completely different experience from the one I'd had when Mia and I traveled together. I dressed for a day of flying in a fleece loungewear set, a cropped puffy vest, and a neck handkerchief (just because it looked cute with my outfit). That was suitable for the cool, dry desert landscape and temperature of the Tucson airport at two-thirty in the morning, but it made no sense in the tropical humidity of an August afternoon in Belize.

Exhausted and overheated, I put the contents of 275 pounds of luggage back together and allowed a porter to drag all four suitcases out to the curb in front of Belize International Airport— or maybe it was the back. I had just landed in a country I'd only ever spent six days in, and I barely knew which end was up.

I'd had a stressful few weeks prior to my departure for Central America, which included securing proper care for Pesto for five months, resigning from my job at just the right time to continue receiving paychecks as long as possible, and packing all of my belongings for a new life on an island. Rasta had been working night shifts seven days a week, so our communication had been much less than what I was used to. When I really needed to hear his voice and see his face, communication dropped off significantly so he could sleep during the day. Being on my own with all the crazy, anxious overthinking had me feeling squirrely (no offense to those frenetic little woodland creatures). I told him it was really important to me that he be there to retrieve me from the dock on the day I arrived—no exceptions, night shifts or not—and he agreed.

I looked down the row of cabs, hoping to see the name of the company I had used five months prior. I had taken a photo of the taxi's license plate and even of me and the driver. When I saw the taxi company attendant, I showed her the selfie I had taken with Lionel, and, recognizing him, she stated he was on his way back to the airport. If I waited, he could take me to the water ferry!

When Lionel arrived twenty minutes later, I enthusiastically greeted him and showed him our photo to help him remember all the fun we'd had the first time around. We made it to my destination with ten minutes to spare, and then about fifty of us loaded onto the water taxi headed to Caye Caulker, where Rasta was waiting. I had only met him in person twice before, for five minutes each, five months ago. Now, I was about to hug him for the first time—and move into an apartment with him. What could possibly go wrong (she said with sarcasm and a wicked smile)?

We stepped off the ferry boat onto the dock, and I looked down the long pier to see Rasta strolling along the other end carrying a bottle of Belikin Stout. He was dressed as I'd expected, in a huge t-shirt (the skinniest guy in XXL!), equally baggy Dickies long shorts, a handkerchief tied around his neck, and beautiful dreadlocks braided down his back. We caught eyes and walked toward each other, me trying not to trip and fall in my platform sandals. After that day, I wouldn't be in anything but flip flops, my primitive island life not conducive to shoes made for sidewalks and hard floors.

Well, shit. We'd actually done it. One chance encounter followed by another had brought us to this moment. All the conversations and planning and curiosity had led us to this spot. I had traveled from my home in the U.S. back to the tiny island of Caye Caulker. There were a lot of missing pieces and moving parts with that approach—you know it and I know it. I would later reflect on this, comparing it to situations in my medical career, years before. If we were working on a patient who needed to be brought back to life and time was of the essence, the medication or procedure usually required a direct, immediate route. We never half-assed a resuscitation. You either do it or you don't. You attempt to save a life or you walk away. There's no in-between. Similarly, this was a high-risk, potentially high-reward situationship. I had followed my heart, allowing my gut instinct to feed me information slowly. But was I letting it fully guide me?

I wanted to find love and keep a relationship with someone, and I was trying to control it by tricking my body, heart, and gut instinct into disregarding some of my own instincts. Because, let's face it, my "normal" instincts had already fed a message to my brain that said moving to a foreign country (and moving in with a man I barely knew) might not be in anyone's best interest, let alone mine.

In the surreal moment of our reunion, I discovered that Rasta gave the best hugs. Though he was so relaxed and a man of few words, I could tell he was a little nervous to finally have me in arm's reach, but we couldn't stop smiling. I had traveled for nine hours across three time zones, so for once I was happy to sit and absorb my new surroundings as the porters unloaded my luggage from the boat.

Rasta got us a taxi (which, on the tiny island, means a golf cart—no cars allowed), and we rode to our new home, a second-story apartment I had found online and secured a lease for, from 2,000 miles away. I had searched for an apartment for us because I knew Rasta wasn't living in a place we—or I, at least—would thrive in. Two months before my arrival, Rasta met with the landlord, Edie, and she and I began speaking over the phone extensively about what I would need to comfortably thrive there. She and I had a lovely connection from the beginning, and we got to know each other through our conversations. The two-level apartment was on the second story, with one bedroom on the main floor and one in the loft. It only had air conditioning in the master bedroom loft and no power outlets in the kitchen, so we had to make toast on the living room floor, but I was happy to have been chosen as the tenant of an apartment that was comfortable enough for me to relax, cook, and write.

Rasta had a little studio apartment about a quarter mile away that didn't have the space or any of the amenities it would take for both of us to live there. I had writing and job hunting to do while simultaneously needing to adjust to tropical island life without throwing all of my coping skills out the window on day one. We agreed to keep his studio apartment in case things didn't work out between us. It's very hard for locals to find affordable housing on the island, which is overrun with tourists and expats (like me). I had more resources than many of the Belizean people, but I wasn't one of those super-rich foreigners who swooped down with bags of money to spend the rest of their days drunk on the beach.

Arriving at the new apartment, I discovered there was no

key waiting for me, no hot water heater, and many other small surprises. For example, I hadn't been aware that, even if you're lucky enough to have a washing machine—which I was—everyone hangs their wet laundry on clotheslines attached to the house or balcony. When Mia and I stayed at that gorgeous resort in March, we had filtered water from our kitchen faucet, air conditioning, hot and cold water, a stackable washer and dryer in the hallway, and every amenity you could imagine in a modern 1200-square-foot condo. I had no idea that most people on the island—and the country as a whole—don't have hot water in their residences.

Even more concerning than the lack of hot water heaters was the absence of any apartment keys. I contacted Edie and was told the keys would be brought in a few hours, so I tried to hide my backpack, which carried my most valuable and expensive belongings, and Rasta and I went out to explore.

It was the rainy season, and bugs are no joke when the humidity is that high. When I started exploring my surroundings, I noticed many tourists walking around with mosquito bite welts, though it was the sandflies that seemed to love my ankles most. It was like a gang initiation—definitely "Bloods," not Crips. The sandflies were so tiny, but their bites seemed stronger than a mosquito's. I grew thankful for the breeze, which seemed to keep the bugs away, but even when I swayed in the balcony hammock, those pesky little assholes would try to land on me, causing me to retreat indoors. Locals told me I would develop some sort of antibody and that the creatures would lose interest in me, as if even the bugs would figure out that I was local and not just a tourist. And eventually they did!

After three days without hot water, I had yet to wash my hair or shave my legs, and I was getting cranky and crusty. The wind was turning my hair into a bird's nest, and, combined with sweat and the tropical heat, my blond mane had taken on a wavy, dog-hair-like texture. Rasta and I both knew there was no point in trying to get too cozy together until my hair had finally been washed and my legs (and other parts) had been shaved. We had been patient for five months already, and Rasta knew I had to get my bearings first—not just from culture or climate shock but from living with a stranger and how that would look moving forward. I had just moved to Central America from a large, modern U.S. city; I had a lot to learn and adapt to.

I have a severe intolerance to being cold. Despite the people with fanatical, almost militant, claims about the healing effects of their frigid practices, ice plunge and ice bath regimens completely agitate me to even think about. I could only stay in the shower for thirty to sixty seconds, and I wondered how long it would take for the cold water to stimulate my vagus nerve and make me pass out on the shower floor. I found a small, on-demand water heater under the cabinet in the bathroom, but it was broken. A few days later, I told Edie I couldn't live that way, and thankfully, she agreed to pay half toward a new water heater. A plumber was there within three hours to install it.

However, the plumber then stood up and announced that the right faucet knob needed to be replaced because it was completely stripped. I asked what type of water would come out of the left one. He replied, "Hot." So, I could have hot water, but I wouldn't have any cold water? Not wanting to be scalded, we needed to turn off the hot water heater as soon as it was installed, at least until we got both faucets functioning. In the end, I took a two-minute shower in bone-chilling water so I could feel clean again, then I returned to the swampy humid air to sweat my nuts off. The following morning, Edie's husband installed two working faucets, and that night I took my first warm shower. Ironically, I eventually found that the climate was indeed too hot and humid for warm showers, so unless I needed to wash my hair, I preferred cold water, just like the locals did.

After more than three months of working twelve-hour night shifts with no days off, Rasta was feeling pretty crazy and exhausted, so we just took everything easy. And, as he and anyone else I ran into tried to explain, that was how things worked on the island. Caye Caulker's official motto is "Go Slow," so we did. Eventually, we found our rhythm, and the closeness of sex was a nice addition to our instant life together.

Even though I kept it at eighty degrees, the air conditioner made Rasta feel sick, so he didn't sleep in the upstairs bedroom with me, opting instead to sleep in the downstairs bedroom with only a fan. I couldn't understand how he was able to sleep so soundly during the day before his night shifts, but he had never lived with air conditioning or hot water. I once witnessed him turn a dusky shade of blue when we were in a cold building. It only took eight minutes before he had to excuse himself and go outside to bask in the heat.

The logistics of my first few days and weeks on the island were not for the weak. I needed to find a company to deliver gas for the tank that powered the stove and another company to deliver five-gallon bottles of drinking water, which I also needed for cooking and brushing my teeth (tap water in Belize was an absolute no-go for me). By contrast, Rasta had lived very simply in his studio apartment, which honestly looked a little like a prison cell with a refrigerator. There were no other appliances, so there was no need for gas, and he used the water jug at work or bought small bottles of water when he needed them at home.

In addition to those factors, I also needed to set up internet and cellular service, which in turn meant purchasing a local cell phone. Anything involving the slightest amount of coordination needed to be addressed, and none of that was as easy to set up as it was in the U.S. Not even close. Living on an island in Central America, power and water could shut off at any moment, and it did on a rather frequent basis. Those were all things I needed to plan for. I bothered my landlord a lot at the very beginning, but I tried to get by fairly self-sufficiently after that. And by "self-sufficiently," I mean that Rasta had to deal with me. Life was very different there than what I was used to.

Prior to the move, one of my dear cousins had asked lots of questions at a family get-together in Wisconsin. He was trying to wrap his brain around all the information about my upcoming trip I'd just laid on them.

He asked, "So, are you going to be living with this guy? Like, will you be roommates?"

"Yes, we will be roommates," I explained. "Roommates who sleep in the same bed ... without pants on." While we didn't end up sleeping in the same bed, I was right about not needing pants!

It was an unorthodox situation for sure, but once we had been cohabitating for a few weeks, things started to feel more natural. I learned and came to understand Rasta's rhythms. We definitely had physical chemistry; he was so gorgeous to me that I could never stop staring at him. He had a mysterious, calm energy that I couldn't figure out sometimes, but it was unique, and I found it attractive, along with the way he spoke and the way he looked at me.

Rasta seemed content with companionship over sexual closeness. He wasn't pawing at me for sex as often as I thought he would, but that was all right with me because I needed to be out of the bedroom often enough to figure out how to live on a tiny Caribbean island. Doing so required pants—or at least a bikini bottom.

With all of the excitement, stress, and planning it had taken to get me on that August 14 flight, followed by the drastic climate change from the desert I had left, my immune system was bound to fuck off. And it sure did. I felt the damp humidity everywhere—in the air, in my body, in all of the fabrics of the house. That's tropical living (and, surprisingly, you do actually get used to it after a while). One of the first body changes I noticed after moving to the Caribbean was that my lower legs and feet swelled by late afternoon, which had never happened to me before. When I finally asked someone about it, they said it was pretty normal among tourists and new locals and that it would go away after a while. And it did.

Soon after arriving on Caye Caulker, I caught a horrible tropical virus, which put exploration and discovery of my new life on hold. I read on local social media forums that some illness was going around, so it was probably inevitable that I caught it. I was bedridden for ten days and, even after that, it took me a week to feel like myself. I could barely get out of bed, wasn't hungry, and had a horrible cough, so I asked Rasta where we could get soup. He brought me soup from a nearby Chinese restaurant and let me rest, which was all I could do. I lived off large containers of vegetable and hot and sour soup for three days at a time, and then he'd go get more when I ran out.

Getting so sick right after I got there was not a great way to start a life with someone, and I barely remember the beginning of that week when I fell ill, but Rasta was extremely patient with me. He was still working with no nights off, so he was sleeping during the day, just like me, and when he woke up in the afternoon before his long work shift, he would get more soup and check on me. He brought me freshly squeezed juices, which were plentiful on the island, and he always tried to get me to drink orange juice. While I was under the weather, my favorites were watermelon, passionfruit, and tamarind.

Once I was feeling better, I made a lot of meals at home for us. Rasta was extremely thin, but he was muscular, one of the strongest men I've ever known. People are built differently in societies where manual labor is required for survival and not many outside businesses or entities provide services to make life easier. I saw how spoiled we were in the U.S. and also how he would eat most anything put in front of him. I suspected he'd spent time being very hungry before. It was a different world ... a third world.

To get all of the necessary groceries, I had to either walk or hire a golf cart taxi. The groceries could get heavy, and the apartment was almost a mile from the nearest grocery store. One day on his way back from work, Rasta came home with a bike for me. He had painted it in swirls of black and blue and placed a basket on the front so I could carry my things more easily. I'd never been a fan of bicycles, but with no scary vehicles around to run us over, bicycling was a safe and fast way to get from one end of the island to the other. Some days, it was just too hot to walk from the apartment to the center of the village. I joked with my friends that I was one of the *Real Housewives of Cayo Caulker*, now that my man had bought a "vehicle" for me.

Thanks to my new ride, groceries were easier to bring home, and more decent meals were prepared. A request for chicken hot dogs and my "famous" salad was even made (Rasta used to see a lot of photos of my salads during our long-distance courtship). He eats like a teenage football player and loves chicken hot dogs and my breakfast sandwiches, which he drowns in a Belizean hot sauce called Marie Sharp's. That sauce is next-level Caribbean habañero hot, and he and all the other locals ate it like it was ketchup. Rasta would eat basically anything except pork—even the conch ceviche I made when someone gave him two pounds of freshly caught conch. What he wouldn't try again, though, was my attempt at a fresh octopus dinner. That wasn't pretty.

One morning, we made guacamole with the largest, craziest shaped avocado I'd ever seen. It was a team effort, as the avocado wasn't quite ripe enough for guac, and our forks were made of poor-quality, very bendy metal. Rasta grabbed a short, heavy glass from the cabinet and then proceeded to smash the avocado. As we finished, I asked him, "Can you believe that six months after we met, we are standing in our apartment, listening to reggae, and making guacamole?" He replied, "For sure, babe. It was meant to be." Obviously, his comment made me smile. It always amused me how few words he used to get his point across, and quite frankly, I liked it.

He was gentle and still seemed a little withdrawn, in keeping with the first time I'd laid eyes on him. But there was something very deep and primal there too. From the occasional stories he shared about his past, I figured he'd had a really hard life and had probably seen some violence. Whether or not he'd had a choice in those events or was defending himself or others, I wasn't sure. But I felt protected by him, especially once people knew that we were together, because men tend to be more aggressive in pursuing single women. Rasta preferred to stick to himself and didn't seem like the type to cause trouble. I figured that was why people just seemed to leave him alone. I would later learn there was more to it than that.

"TROUBLE IS JUST LIKE LOVE, AFTER ALL; IT COMES IN UNANNOUNCED AND TAKES OVER BEFORE YOU'VE HAD A CHANCE TO RECONSIDER, OR EVEN TO THINK."

— *Alice Hoffman*

chapter four

STORM WARNING

Three weeks after arriving, I was mostly recovered and could shift my focus back to exploring my surroundings. Third-world country or not, island life is not for everyone. It would take time to figure out how everything worked and meet more people, hunt for healthy food items, and get my life there set up comfortably.

Over and over, I was reminded that island life is fantastic for ten days at a crack while staying at luxury resorts, but for residents—native or foreign—living like a local is incredibly tough. The minuscule island was like a fishbowl, at least in terms of how gossip circulates. Imagine living in a small town where everyone is in everyone else's business *and* you're surrounded by water. There was no escape.

We really see what we're made of when we're challenged or in a state of discomfort after deviating from our homeostasis. Add in trying to learn new things and level out while keeping our hearts open and soft to what's meant for us and filtering out the dangerous or misaligned. Bloody hell.

Goddammit, the growth I experienced while being physically uncomfortable in this new living situation was astounding.

Not just once I got to the island but even before that, going through my belongings and trying to fit much of my life into four suitcases and a single backpack—that process can cause a lot of discomfort when you come from Western culture and are fortunate enough to be relatively middle class. I had "stuff," and I like nice things, but I had noticed in the last few years that I frequently felt stifled, as if there were too many things in my tiny house, even though I didn't seem to collect items or decorate as much as other people I knew. I hadn't felt a sense of permanence in many of the places I'd lived in and never hung art or decor on the walls. Either that, or I'm just too fucking lazy to climb a ladder with a ruler and a nail.

Coming straight from ten years in the Sonoran desert, the island's tropical surroundings were naturally uncomfortable yet captivating, and even the culture was different from what I was used to. While nearly everyone in Belize spoke English, most conversation around me was done in Kriol, not much of which is understandable to non-natives. So many parts of daily life I used to navigate with so much ease now required a lot of thought in order to figure out how to accomplish whatever it was I needed to do.

This journey was more intense and profound during times when I really had to dig deep within myself or get resourceful with my surroundings. Growth doesn't usually happen when we're comfy and cozy. I had beautiful moments with new people from all cultures, backgrounds, and walks of life, but it wasn't always easy to find common ground with someone who grew up and lived completely differently from me. Interacting with new people can be challenging, whether they're strangers in a water taxi or the hot Caribbean stranger you're living with. It forces us to confront things within ourselves that we thought were normal and acceptable but that another part of the world might think are strange.

Switching up living environments, I learned not only about others but also about myself. The situation and location in Belize meant that everyday life was more challenging at even an elemental level. The things most of us take for granted in the U.S. were not even options where I had landed. Living in the Caribbean meant that almost no one was on, or at least stuck to, a schedule of any kind. Things moved slower, and people were more relaxed about situations that often bend us out of shape in Western culture. Compared to any location I'd lived in before, I was confronted with inconvenient occurrences like power outages and clean water shortages, not to mention the hurricanes and crocodiles!

Rules and laws (what laws?) were also different. Getting my passport stamped for permission to stay in Belize involved taking a boat north every thirty days to the city of San Pedro on the island of Ambergris Caye, which housed the Immigration and Customs Office. The options were to pay a hundred dollars a month doing it this way, or else enter a different country—the closest being Guatemala or Mexico—and return with a fresh stamp. While recovering from being sick, the trip to San Pedro was something I had to get organized and mapped out.

At about the four-week point, Rasta and I started having problems. At first, I thought he was just tired because of his insane overnight work schedule, but I was starting to notice differences in how we maneuvered things at home as well. He couldn't be still unless he was asleep or smoking weed, and since our landlord didn't allow smoking on the premises, he'd have to step away and come back home at regular intervals. I started to wonder if he actually had anxiety and only came across so chill because of the self-medication wrapped in a tobacco leaf. This was just one of a number of odd little things, which I had initially attributed to cultural differences but started to worry might be indicative of bigger issues.

By this point, I'd heard several women's horror stories about local men. Of course, there are scary assholes everywhere and from every country, but here I was suddenly exposed to what seemed to be a higher-than-normal concentration per capita. It wasn't just that local men tended to have a wife, a girlfriend, *and* a side chick but also that there was significant domestic abuse in male-female relationships.

If that weren't enough dysfunction, I learned that it was also quite normal for women to sleep with several men to get their bills paid: one partner would pay a cell phone bill, another dalliance would handle utilities, et cetera. Sugar baby and sugar daddy relationships exist with similar arrangements in the U.S., but in Belize they seemed to be born out of more dire need. I preferred to stay in the cougar enclosure of the relationship zoo. (This cougar wants to continue dating younger lion cubs, *not* sugar daddies—we're not there yet!). As independent as I was, I also wanted to be especially respectful in our new relationship. Rasta seemed more jealous and possessive than other men I'd known, but the initial challenges we faced paled in comparison to the other experiences I'd heard about. So, I tried to compromise and reassure him, hoping he would see how trustworthy and loyal I was by nature.

I'm a light sleeper, and Rasta would wake me up at all hours of the night, turning on the kitchen light and opening and closing the refrigerator. I knew he stood in the hot, humid Caribbean weather for both his day and night shifts, so I attributed his hunger and thirst to that and his difficult work schedule. But as we continued living together, I came to recognize and describe his behavior this way: "Living with Rasta is like living with a slightly tamed wild animal—sweet, but still a bit wild." No truer words could have summed it up. Of course, he still looked a little untamed as well, which was also part of why I was so attracted to him.

On Monday afternoon, the day before heading to San Pedro to visit the Immigration and Customs Office and explore Belize a bit more, I left the cafe where I often sat and wrote. Incredibly hungry and knowing I wouldn't make it home before a downpour of rain I saw coming, I parked my bike and went in to grab my favorite meal at a nearby restaurant, conch fritters. After ordering, the woman seated alone at the table next to mine smiled really big and asked if I lived on the island.

I wasn't sure if it was the fading bug bites, the start of an all-over tan, or maybe even the look on my face that tipped her off, but you can tell when someone is living on the island. Visitors usually have a specific appearance, wide-eyed and looking lost. Anyway, I told this woman, Kari, that I did live there, and she seemed excited that I was local. We chatted about how long she'd been living in Belize, and I asked her a lot of questions.

She was an accountant who worked from home and had a house in San Ignacio but had been living on Caye Caulker for a couple of years. She was three days away from returning to her home on the mainland. Years ago, she had met a Belizean man back home in Texas, then married and followed him to Central America. Things didn't work out, but she stayed.

Kari was very friendly, but she was a little "off." I couldn't put a distinct reason to my gut feeling about her, but I trusted that my gut was almost never wrong (when I was listening to it, at least). I asked for her contact information anyway, in case I had random questions about maneuvering through life here, even if in the long run she might not be someone who would help with my survival needs if any arose.

Let's face it: going to a tiny foreign island to live with a man you've only known for five months (most of which took place over the phone) can yield some surprises—or worse. It was probably the craziest leap of faith I could have taken. Yet, I discovered just how risky it was only once I'd lived in Belize for a while, though not in the obvious stranger danger way you're probably thinking. Based on what I'd seen and heard, I was under the impression that I had moved in with quite possibly the safest, gentlest man on the island. But "safe" and "gentle" are subjective, aren't they?

Sadly, they're also transmutable. Things change. Now, you and I are likely both asking, did my gut *really* tell me that moving to Belize and cohabitating with a virtual stranger might not be the smartest choice? Well, sure, there were moments when I thought—from a logical, logistical, prudent level—that my decision wasn't the safest or the smartest. But I was done with living smart and safe (most of the time). I felt too tamed. I needed to break free to reclaim a little wild in any way I could, and this was the way I chose. The Universe knew what she was doing. In order to regain my wildness, I had to be on that island. I had to go to Belize before I could get to the next destination on this journey.

I told Kari the story about how I met and moved in with Rasta. When I showed her a photo of us, she exclaimed loudly, as if she recognized him. Then, she quickly pivoted to a loud tirade about how the local men were all the same. Her reaction to the photo really had me worried, and I begged her to tell me specifics about Rasta if she had any. She brushed me off, continuing to carry on with her dramatics.

"Look," I said. "I am in a relationship with this person. If you have information that I need to know, please tell me now!" I have no earthly idea why, but she refused to say more, even after her strong reaction suggested she might know potentially vital information that might affect my well-being and wouldn't cost her anything to share. I had only eaten part of my meal, and I was seriously freaked out by what Kari was and wasn't saying. Part of me thought this woman was probably full of shit, but still being new to the country, the island, and the relationship, meeting her caught me a certain way. Sisters, women need to look out for each other. You'd better believe that if I had information that would keep you safe from another human or situation, I would sing like a tipsy canary.

Kari went off to drink with a whole table of tanned, leathery-skinned expats like herself, and I paid for my meal and got up to leave, just wanting to be back home. Knowing Rasta was sleeping for his night shift at my apartment, there was no way I was about to wake him up to ask about this crazy woman I had just met. I had, however, snuck a photo of her and was intent on showing him later, just to see his reaction.

Outside, the rain was coming down harder than I'd ever seen, and my bike had been knocked over onto a concrete block by the weather. I stood it back up and walked it around the corner with my heavy backpack. As I steered toward the road, the handlebars disconnected, and the bike fell over again. Just weeks beforehand, I had been living with my cat in a little rented casita in the Southwest desert, not far from Mexico. I drove a new SUV, went Latin dancing with friends four nights a week, and had unlimited resources for groceries, shopping, and healthcare. Now, I was living on a tiny island in a developing country with a quiet, antisocial local who very likely smoked too much weed, and my vehicle—the sweet little blue and black bicycle with the basket in front—had just lost its entire steering column. In the back of my mind (or maybe in my gut), I felt that these experiences and adventures were all teaching me valuable lessons, as if something—maybe Spirit or Universe, I wasn't sure—was trying to tell me to "listen and learn" because I would need to be paying attention. Hopefully, I would be able to integrate and learn from the lessons coming my way.

On Tuesday morning, Rasta and I took the water taxi to San Pedro, and from San Pedro, we would bypass Caye Caulker and take the water taxi to visit Belize City. It was time I toured the mainland, and Rasta needed to get a break from the island. Our five days on the mainland were sort of a kamikaze mission because most of Central America and other parts of the Caribbean were getting hit with record rains and flooding, making it incredibly difficult to travel (or even leave the house). There was no way to predict if the weather would clear or hold long enough to enjoy any sightseeing.

In spite of the tricky weather, we traveled to the mainland, where we stayed in nice lodging but would take buses rather than renting a car. It was a very confusing system, though. I couldn't find any rhyme or reason to these bus routes with little waiting areas littered sporadically alongside rural roads. The thing was, you couldn't always get on one bus and go all the way to your destination; you often had to get off one bus and hop onto another, making a much longer trip than you'd think would be possible for such a small country. Rasta had an idea as to how the transportation operated in Belize, but it had been years since he'd traveled anywhere significant outside of Caye Caulker, so we relied on random strangers to help us get where we needed to go.

For the most part, everyone we asked was very helpful. But

even locals were sometimes mystified about certain aspects of how things worked in their homeland, and they almost always spoke Belizean Kriol, so I was in the dark about what was being said most of the time. It was a miracle that the bus drivers and assistants even knew where to pick up and drop off passengers. I was forced to follow Rasta, and, true to form, when I had questions, he would respond, "Why don't you just trust me?" Well, first off, sir, you can barely keep your baggy pants from falling off that narrow ass, so how can I trust you to catch a bus? I couldn't deny, though, that I did need to trust. Life there demanded I do so, to trust rather than be rushed or worried, as was my tendency.

We did manage to have some fun moments, though, like when Rasta ordered what he thought was an iced coffee (which he had recently discovered and found highly delicious) but received an iced boba tea. It turned out that having big black balls in his drinks wasn't for him—fair enough. But it certainly wasn't all fun times, interesting sights, and boba tea. Rasta and I got on each other's nerves, for sure. Our fundamental differences were highlighted at almost every turn.

In San Ignacio, we caught a taxi to visit an ancient Mayan temple. Inside the "vehicle," every single warning light made for that particular year of Nissan was illuminated on its dashboard. If a light came on in my Nissan SUV, I'd skip the maintenance manual and text my service advisor at the car dealership, who would either explain what it was and how to fix it or tell me to come in right away. This car, on the other hand, did not appear to be roadworthy. Seriously, the dashboard was lit up like a Christmas tree. A very different approach to car ownership and maintenance!

I reached where one normally finds a seatbelt and didn't

feel one. I must have whispered something to Rasta because the driver laughed and piped up: "This is Belize! You don't need no seat belts." Then, he took us to a remote spot outside of town, where a couple of cars were parked, and Rasta bought some weed. We continued driving as he rolled and lit a joint in the backseat. I don't normally smoke weed, but I didn't have a job that would drug test me (or any job, for that matter) and was living a wild Caribbean existence, so I thought I might as well embrace that. I mean, it was much more dangerous not to wear a seatbelt than to smoke a joint, and I knew Rasta wouldn't give me something he thought would be too strong for me.

Rasta continually insisted I "not be so hype." I'd learned quite a bit by then about taking life and situations easier, but I was admittedly still much more "hype" than a Caribbean stoner. While I could stand to be more chill, I would never operate at his pace unless I was heavily sedated. He was always wanting me just to go with the flow, to "go slow." I could see how a life without expectations of how something would turn out was so much easier, but I had yet to come close to mastering it.

I was trying so hard to slow down (that statement alone is proof that I wasn't succeeding), but it was so hard when I was living my greatest nightmare: cars with inoperable seatbelts and buses full of people, all of whom seem to be listening to music, playing videos, or having phone conversations loud enough to compete with the music overhead. Not to mention the occasional unhappy child or two.

All this reminded me of a concept I'd been introduced to twenty years prior, back when I was volunteering at a local dog rescue organization. A woman whose family was going to adopt a sweet dog suggested after only thirty minutes of speaking together that it seemed like I might be what was called a "highly sensitive person" (HSP). The woman, a clinical psychologist, explained that this personality type was becoming more acknowledged and was typically attributed to highly intelligent people who seek out opportunities to do deep work. HSPs are often academics, artists, researchers, and scientists. And can you guess what tends to trigger HSPs? Overstimulation.

Those of us with this particular brand of "quirkiness" can be easily overwhelmed by sights, sounds, and even textures, causing distress or anxiety. For example, HSPs might feel overwhelmed when their environment is too noisy, bright, cold, or crowded, surrounded by chatter, chaos, and clutter. So, yes. I am more than likely an HSP. I had also at times been called "neurodivergent." I guess that's today's politically correct way to say "you're weird." I'd rather not be called neurodivergent, unless it's used to mean I'm some sort of supernatural creature like a vampire or a violent fairy.

After a few days on the mainland and an excursion to Placencia Caye, we made our way to the dock to catch our water taxi back home. We made it to the dock with an hour to kill, and I was starving, so Rasta went to find some fruit and chips for us. Once he came back with food, he issued one of his "I'll be right back" notifications and disappeared, heading away from the dock. I had learned by now that this was normal for him. He wouldn't usually tell me where he was going and often just muttered, "I'll be right back." I never knew if he was going to take a pee or smoke a joint, but he was a grown man, and I wasn't babysitting anyone. Do what you gotta do. I just didn't want to miss that water taxi, as I knew it would be two hours until the next one.

I ate by myself and then walked over to a man sitting at a table with a chessboard. He was an odd-looking older gentleman who didn't seem very keen on personal hygiene, with long, dirty nails and clothes that probably hadn't been washed in a while. We're all pretty disheveled after living a bit primitively in the excess humidity and heat, but this guy looked like he was feeling excess everything (I was grateful I couldn't smell him). I tried to play chess with him, but he was making up all kinds of strange rules. I had forgotten most of the rules myself, but I'd bet money this guy didn't know what the heck he was doing either. It was the most frustrating game I'd ever played. Obviously, I lost since I didn't even know what game we ended up playing.

Finally, I saw Rasta's tall, dark figure rounding the corner toward the dock with just minutes to spare before our boat was due to arrive. Strolling. Hot as fuck. Slow as a turtle. Caribbean life is so laid-back and chill that there's almost never a sense of urgency, but this was not the moment I wanted to just chill and take a gamble. Realizing I had no control over the boat or Rasta, I started to get riled up, or "spicy," as he often called me.

I didn't bother hiding my irritation when I asked him what the fuck he was doing that made us almost miss the boat (I knew Belizean men were used to women speaking to them that way, but it hadn't occurred to me to wonder whether the women who did so usually got away with it). Rasta wasn't thrilled with my tone. He pointed to a shack with a tiny dock where random strangers were sitting outside. It was clear that Rasta had gone off to smoke weed at some sketchy house. Even if Belizeans always seem to somehow know each other, I had no idea if he actually knew these people or could just tell they'd have a lighter for him to borrow. Regardless, he'd left me to fend for myself as I waited for the boat.

Rasta then angrily launched into some jealous diatribe about this gross, crusty old dude I was playing chess with. He acted like I had given him a lap dance while Rasta was away. I was flab-bergasted—again with the extreme jealousy. I had gathered that his jealousy seemed to be deep insecurity stemming from, at the very least, his girlfriend before me. Addicted to drugs and with no aim in life, she was apparently willing to do whatever it took and with whomever just to score some drugs. It made sense, but it was no excuse.

I wasn't used to that kind of behavior. It made me feel trapped and caged, and I think some of it was rubbing off on me. His jealousy when I talked to other people (especially men), even if I was just asking for directions or politely saying hello, was becoming more and more apparent. It was starting to seem like he was always suspicious of me and who I was talking to, which seemed childish and surpassed healthy boundaries of affection. Rasta often showed the kind of protectiveness a man demon-strates around the woman he loves, but I was also starting to see this other side: immature, jealous, and unnecessarily paranoid.

My experience with Rasta was just like that game of chess. There just wasn't enough emotional intelligence or rational thought for two people to play a game that required intellectual reasoning. It was like playing chess with someone who only knew how to play checkers—or who just made up the rules as they went and never bothered to explain them to the other participant.

I had expected Rasta to be a man, but his jealous attitude and possessive behavior made me feel like a child. No one could tell me what to do or who to talk to. I needed to be free to travel where I wanted and interact with whomever I chose. Deep down in my gut, I was starting to wonder if this kind of behavior was worse than simply making me feel caged. I worried about its potential to be more than inappropriate and unacceptable, that it had the potential to be dangerous. While boarding the water taxi, I knew my relationship with Rasta needed to end. He was too unstable.

Disgruntled, we both climbed aboard and sat together for just a few minutes before he relocated to the far side. When we arrived at the island, Rasta walked off the boat and didn't even look back to see where I was. When I caught up to him, he was silent and incredibly pissed off. I asked him what the hell that was back at the dock, but his explanation made no sense. We were both quiet for a moment, and then Rasta asked if he could carry my backpack. I said "no" and picked up my pace as we continued along the beach toward our apartment, fed up with the heat as well as our interaction. That seemed to anger him even more, and he veered up ahead and disappeared in another direction.

For the next three days, Rasta didn't show up and wouldn't answer any of my messages or calls. While I knew where his apartment was, it wasn't in a great location, and I didn't want to go hunting him down there. Why would I, anyway? He had shown his blatant immaturity when, instead of talking through an issue, he just ran away. That was something I couldn't tolerate.

Those days without any contact felt horrible. I was and always would be a badass, but I push through a lot of fears to be that way—fears that I carry from childhood and beyond. I am fearful, but I "do the thing" anyway. Sometimes, though, I get overwhelmed and everything adds up. Well, this was one of those times. I had been figuring out a lot on my own since arriving, but I still felt that Rasta was protecting me. He was like my pot-smoking, saggy-pants and double-boxers-wearing ambassador, a buffer that kept me from being hit head-on with the unfamiliar nuances of living abroad. While I had come to Belize of my own volition, some of what brought me there when it did was my desire to see where this relationship with Rasta would go. Now unsure what my next move should be, I cried a lot and didn't get out of bed for a whole day and night. I didn't know what the hell he was doing or thinking, and I certainly didn't know how to handle this unexpected situation. I was scared and sad.

We don't have all the answers, but we figure out what to do anyway. Sometimes we just have to work through it to get to the other side. When Rasta finally returned my messages, I found out that he had stormed off because he didn't appreciate my angry tone and hadn't wanted to trail behind me as we walked back to the apartment (What, he couldn't walk any faster?!). Regardless of the explanation, disappearing from your romantic partner with absolutely no contact for days told me everything I needed to know. I had only been in his country for a short time, yet a mere exchange of harsh words between us was enough for him to disappear and leave me to fend for myself. Luckily, I'm resourceful, but that doesn't excuse him abandoning me just because we both got frustrated. If we as adults couldn't talk through our issues to find some common ground and mutual respect, there was no point in continuing that type of relationship.

The truth is, my gut was starting to work as it should, outweighing all the other body parts (in other words, my brain, heart, and vagina were finally being told to "shut the hell up" in order for me to start protecting myself). It was time to think clearly and logically and to focus on goals other than being in love and having an epic love story to tell about it.

I'm all about the feelings and the connection—even better if it comes with a story or meet-cute that makes people say, "Seriously?! You did what?! With who?!" While that's not why I did what I did, any situation with a set-up that moves my heart captivates me. I mean, meeting a stranger in a foreign land and seeing where our hearts would take us was much more my style than saying, "We're high school sweethearts. I was a cheerleader, and Ken was captain of the football team." That kind of story would never be enough to settle my heart and soul, the essential duo that is boundlessly curious and so great at seeking. I wouldn't want to force them to settle in a way they didn't want to.

After talking again, I told Rasta we were through and asked him to move out, saying that we could be friends but would never be a couple again. It took him weeks to finally retrieve all of his belongings from my apartment, but I didn't waver. I could sense something—a lot of something—in Rasta's behavior over those three days spent apart.

During that time, I tried to continue exploring the island and writing, taking in as much as I could while dealing with frustrations from Rasta. He constantly asked me who I was talking to or interacting with, even after I had broken up with him. I was trying to be friends with him by keeping the lines of communication open, but he wanted to know my whereabouts and who I was interacting with and started accusing me of having inappropriate relationships with half the guys on the island. If I mentioned I had spoken with a man while I was out running errands—whether it was a tour guide, a store owner, or an old man on the city council—I got questions.

I wasn't used to that level of scrutiny or insecurity from anyone. None of my other relationships were built that way. I could go where I wanted, say what I wanted, talk to whomever I wanted, and certainly wear whatever I wanted. Rasta made it seem like that was all up for debate, and it only escalated.

"IT IS WORSE TO STAY WHERE
ONE DOES NOT BELONG AT ALL
THAN TO WANDER ABOUT LOST
FOR A WHILE AND LOOKING
FOR THE PSYCHIC AND SOULFUL
KINSHIP ONE REQUIRES."

— *Clarissa Pinkola Estés*

chapter five

WHEN I WAS STILL TAME

About eighteen years ago, I was living in Madison, Wisconsin, with my then-husband and our four (soon to be five) adopted chihuahuas. My so-called "traditional life" was never classified as normal by most people's standards probably because I was never meant to be traditional or "normal," but it was the closest I'd ever get to a typical, ordinary life. I met my ex-husband skydiving when he was thirty-eight and I was twenty-five. Three months later, Liam and I were engaged, and after another two months, married. For our wedding, Liam and I jumped out of an airplane together under one big chute, right after the officiant.

Despite our distinct romantic pasts, my husband and I came from similar cultures and mindsets, along with similar concepts of what love and monogamy looked like. We both believed there was one person with whom you could build a life, "till death did us part." There was one caveat: I didn't actually believe in marriage. I believed in monogamy and cohabitating, but the meaning of marriage in the religious sense—or even the legal sense—was unimportant to me. If anything, it was a detractor.

Liam's parents had been married for over fifty years and counting. While my parents were divorced, they shared a set of very conservative Christian beliefs. Because they, and my even more conservative paternal grandmother, were still living, I thought that "living in sin" would be too much for them to process. Liam was happy to enter into marriage, so we went for it.

Up until then, I had been dating models, dancers, and bodybuilders—people I considered "pretty boys." There was also the occasional doctor or healthcare worker, as I worked long hours in hospitals, and most of them were also easy on the eyes (though, more often than not, also pretty two-dimensional). With Liam, it was different. While he wasn't unattractive, what drew me to him most was his personality, sense of humor, quick wit, and intelligence. He could build anything, fix anything, and persuade groups of people (even if they were intoxicated) to cooperate and collaborate. He probably would have made a fantastic cult leader, though, thank goodness, he never tried that.

When I met him, Liam was revered at the skydiving dropzone. It was wondrous to watch. He had this aura and energy about him that made people respect him. He didn't demand it; it was just given to him. From the moment we met, I felt as if I'd known him forever, and I felt instantly comfortable and very safe in his presence. I knew he would keep me safe, and I wasn't wrong.

When we were first dating, I would drive down from Wisconsin, where I lived at the time, to Illinois, where he lived, to spend the weekends together. Sometimes we'd head to the dropzone south of Chicago to party with our friends and skydive. I mostly socialized on the sidelines and only jumped on rare occasions and with lots of supervision. I was introduced to all of his friends, a dynamic, diverse group of people who just wanted to have fun and jump out of airplanes—no drama (unless you consider spending the day jumping out of airplanes dramatic).

Skydivers are a very touchy-feely group and have been known to switch romantic partners as fast as Hollywood celebrities. We were always hugging each other on the ground, in the air, by a bonfire.

The friend group was made up of people of all ages, including engineers, computer geeks, artists, medical professionals, hippies (or less conventionally employed people), and, of course, some seriously talented airplane pilots. One of my favorites in the group was James, the most laid-back, fun-loving, go-with-the-flow person I'd ever met. Like Liam, he was a military veteran, and James had served as an officer on several active duty tours in the Middle East. But you'd never know it, watching him bounce out to the jump plane in tie-dyed shorts and a colorful canopy rig. James was magnetic, always ready with a smile and a huge hug, and everyone loved him. It was easy to see how he and Liam had become such good friends.

One weekend early on in our relationship, we were grabbing pizza slices in the food court at a Chicago shopping mall when a man came up and excitedly greeted Liam. I was holding my pizza, wondering when I could dig into it, when I heard the guy say, "It's great to see you! When did you get out?" Now, I'd watched enough TV to know he wasn't asking when Liam had gotten out of medical school, and I had questions but waited until we were back in the truck to ask them. He explained the situation to me, and I thanked him for telling me but also explained I would need proof that everything went down the way he said it did. The situation and the story surrounding it were that serious.

A few weeks later at Liam's parents' house, I saw some of the newspaper clippings surrounding the event that had caused Liam's incarceration. His parents interjected with some of their own recollections from that painful time. I knew it must have been heartbreaking for any loved one to worry and wait while someone they love is locked up in a maximum security prison. The stories that man can tell, and the lives he was able to help and influence while on the inside, were admirable. He had a way about him, an ability to help, be an advocate, and make a difference to those who needed it most. I hadn't been wrong about him.

Liam had lived a hard life for some time (and he was also a cigarette smoker), and it showed. He had that rough, tough-biker look. He'd been in the Marine Corps and then became a one-percent biker (think, biker gangs like Hell's Angels), but he was kind and thoughtful. He reminded me of Kris Kristofferson in *Blade* or Sam Elliott in *Roadhouse*. In both movies, these salt-and-pepper-haired gentlemen kicked ass for the greater good. Liam always fought for the underdog: women, children, animals—those who couldn't advocate for themselves. I'd seen him step in and be a champion in situations that seemed small but made a big impact on the person or creature he was helping. He had a calm, masculine energy that I was drawn to, but he was also a very free spirit who exhibited wild, spontaneous tendencies.

I really liked having Liam in my life. Very soon after we met, he became my best friend. We texted and talked on the phone constantly. He was my sounding board and my confidant who made me feel safe and seen, but I wasn't sure if I had romantic feelings for him. Still, the thought of not having him in my life— or worse, having to deal with another woman in his—was not a scenario I wanted to encounter. So, one night when I was visiting him in Illinois, I got up the courage to look at him and say, "Listen, I don't know that I can live with you. I don't know that I can live with anyone. But I do know that I can't live without you." Two months later, we were married. And that's how it started.

Neither one of us wanted children, but very soon after

getting married, we got our "kids" by rescuing a series of fur kids until we had a weird little pack of five chihuahuas (yes, five), a Siberian Husky-Great Pyrenees mix, and the most glorious, once-feral farm cat the world would ever see. We had adopted each of the little creatures (I guess "adopted" is already implied since I didn't pop these babies out of my own body) from various animal welfare organizations, and, in the case of my favorite— the sweet, naive ginger-haired one—through word of mouth. I usually worked only three hospital shifts per week as a respiratory therapist, and I had a lot of free time on my hands, which I spent with them, with Liam, or on my own, doing basically whatever I wanted.

Before the cat came onto the scene and I realized that cats are way more awesome, I immersed myself in pet parenthood and all things *dog*. Cats were the only pets I'd had as a child since we weren't allowed to have indoor pets, according to my farmer dad. Stray mama cats would have their kittens in our dairy cow barn, and I'd sit for hours trying to tame these hissing, feral furballs. Kittens are born ready to cut a bitch, whereas puppies are ready to wear hats and eat snacks out of your hands.

All six of our dogs arrived to us already tame, with no need to teach them how to live in a house amongst humans. We just had the difficult task of learning all their little personalities and quirks as they arrived one by one and saw how the pack dynamics changed as each one moved in. Because I was denied indoor pets as a child, which caused an inexplicable void, it sort of made sense that as an adult I'd go overboard with how many animals I cohabitated with.

Humans were fine and all, but from a very young age, I was much more comforted by the presence of animals. Their energy and behavior seemed to ground me, but I never stopped to think about how or why I needed that. I just knew that I had an affinity for them, and they seemed to have one for me as well. It was mostly mammals that I realized I had a deep connection with, as they were what I was most exposed to from growing up in the rural Midwest. I was always fearful and mistrusting of birds and snakes. Not to throw anyone under the bus for that, but my sweet little mama always had a deep fear of both (and also of me getting kidnapped, molested, or murdered, or that I wasn't wearing sunscreen, or that I would otherwise somehow meet my demise while running casual Saturday errands). My mom was, and still is, overprotective of me. It was sort of understandable when I was seven years old, but at forty-nine it became a teeny bit excessive. Hey, at least I know she really cares.

I was fortunate to have had parents who made sure I was safe and taken care of. But, living in a very conservative religious household in rural Wisconsin, I was tamed too far. They—*we*—had overcorrected. I say "we" because, as stubborn and independent as I was as a child, I was still a child. There wasn't much of anything wild in my early years, except for those feral kittens I tirelessly tamed in the haymow of our barn.

Because of my parents' stance, we lived a rather sedate, average life of church once or twice a week and not too many social outlets other than an occasional sleepover with my best friend. Sometimes, my brother and I would go on afternoon fishing trips to a pond or lake with my dad, and our family of four took frequent weekend trips north to my paternal grandparents' house for overnight stays with Sunday church visits and huge homemade meals before the long drive back home.

It was the kind of familial situation that assumed we'd go to college and then get married and have kids. My parents may not have definitively said so, but I don't remember anyone cheering me on when I wanted to be a veterinarian or astronaut either. The thing is, I assumed love was in my cards, but I had no idea what it would look like. At a very young age, I had crushes on cute young boys and even handsome, fully grown men. I would see them at church, local baseball games, restaurants, or random gatherings and maybe on TV. I knew what I thought was nice looking, and age didn't seem to matter.

As for becoming a parent one day, I didn't even like children when I *was* one, and I certainly didn't want to have any. Ever. Even physically, I never wanted to feel what it was like for my body to be pregnant. I mean, I was skinny and got motion sick at the slightest inconvenience—not a great setup for someone who's trying to incubate a kid in their personal oven for nine months. Fortunately, I dodged that bullet (though I have no idea how because it certainly wasn't from having safe sex).

The Christian sex-education book my mom gave me wasn't going to explain love or sex, which is no surprise, considering that strict Christians don't tend to hand out pornographic magazines and ask you to take notes for a pop quiz later. That would have been something. I was so sheltered from outside influences, including television and movies, that one time my mom got very upset just because I had watched *Dirty Dancing,* starring Patrick Swayze, with a church friend. I promise you (and my mother) that, of all the things I've seen and done in this life, it was absolutely not watching *Dirty Dancing* at age twelve that traumatized me. If anything, what still strikes fear and discomfort is the memory of the witch and evil monkeys in *The Wizard of Oz.* Something about those witch feet under the house or perhaps the pack of monkeys flying off to do nefarious things made a more jarring impact than Patrick's gyrating hips.

Due to the nature of the movies and television shows I was

allowed to watch, I had always bought into the kind of story where men and women overcome all odds to find true love and a happy ending. That's what I get for watching all of those Disney movies. I always wanted that type of powerful, devoted love that keeps you up at night and lights your heart and soul on fire.

Then I grew up, and things got more complicated because love and passion and relationships have to endure for longer than a two-hour feature film. Turns out those idiots writing movie scripts are taking us on a roller coaster of emotions that can actually span sixty years. Off the movie screen, I realized emotions and feelings were much more complex and complicated. I discovered that my beliefs about romantic relationships, love, sex, soulmates, and everything related to the subject were shifting and changing the older I got.

The last few years Liam and I lived in Wisconsin, we had three dogs left and a hobby farm where I milked a couple of goats and had a llama, some chickens, a mini horse, and three adorable barn cats. One day, an extremely wild stray cat showed up on my hobby farm. I named him Pesto, in keeping with the running theme (we already had barn cats named Pork Chop, Puddin', and Pot Pie—don't ask). Pesto wouldn't let humans get within fifty feet of him, but he was insistent on trying to help himself to my beloved barn cats' food as well as picking fights with them. Therefore, I was insistent on taming him. So, for the next six months, I did just that.

Pesto was so wild, yet he seemed to want to stay close to me once we finally broke the ice. He had been afraid of people for so long that his instinct was to run away. He was more feral than any of the barn cats I had tamed as a child, his spirit so wild that it seemed he had always been on the run. But I was patient with him, and he allowed me to tame him into domestic-ness.

I don't know if anyone else would have ended up with the relationship Pesto and I have. After a successful neuter and back leg amputation due to pre-existing injury, it became clear Pesto was no longer the wild animal who lived in the woods. At least ninety-nine percent tamed, Pesto would lie next to me in the bed as I kissed his squishy body, once in a while noticing a tiny, dark brown crumb that he'd left behind. I had no idea whether it was a piece of cookie, pebbles of litter he'd tracked in, or, worse, a dried-up turd that had clung to his cheeks for dear life only to fall onto my $300 linen sheets. Fuck this kid.

Turns out being feral wasn't in his stars, and true to form, he was reborn into a life he was more suited for. He wouldn't survive on his own at that point, and we had to adopt him and become his guardians. He was meant to find me, and it was clear that he really enjoyed the urban life of a domestic prince, happily becoming part of a weird little dog pack.

Fourteen years into the marriage, Liam and I were walking our last two dogs, Gunnar and Wulf. My darling Loki had passed away just twelve hours after my fortieth birthday party, one month prior. Loki was a five-pound rescue dog whose long, white and tan hair could stand in a mohawk with a mere flip of your hands. He was a little ladies' man who loved to be held like a human baby and seemed more than comfy lying up against a set of boobs—any set of boobs would do. When Loki passed, it really took a chunk of my heart, and in the weeks that followed, I realized how unhappy I was.

Liam and I used to be free-spirited and spontaneous people, but we had become more settled over time, most likely out of my need to feel stable and secure, financially or otherwise. I was a worrier by nature, and I had not only myself but also a husband and three to five furry dependents to consider at all times, and I was starting to realize how much it weighed on me. A lot. Liam's attitude was much more laidback than mine, which caused some of my anxieties to kick into overdrive with each year that passed. We had settled into a routine, and it seemed the only things that brought me joy were those animals. I could feel there was more for me out there, though.

I didn't have the peace I was craving, or maybe it was freedom I was missing. Either way, I was spending a lot of time wondering "what if," waiting for my life to change, and unsure if it ever would. But there was another issue: due to my husband's history, I'd gotten it into my head that if I either left or cheated on Liam, he might snap. Sounds dramatic, but remember: perception is reality. In truth, my husband had never even raised his voice to me during the fifteen years I'd known him, but with my knowledge of his outlaw past and the nature of my own extreme thought processes, I worried I might be in grave danger. But I also knew I wasn't fully living and was destined for more. I could feel it. I didn't have a death wish, but I finally spoke up.

When we got back to our front door, I stepped inside and said to him, "How happy are you in this marriage? I'm not very happy." Liam was his usual calm self, though I could see the shock on his face. It clearly blindsided him initially, though deep down we both knew our marriage was far from perfect or even satisfying. We proceeded to have a deep, teary, three hour conversation. By the time we were done, some of the chaotic feelings, shock, and intense emotions had passed, most likely from sheer mental exhaustion. One of us finally cracked a semblance of a joke (we both have incredible senses of humor in most situations, despite all odds), and then we realized it was late in the evening.

The other thing we realized, oddly, was that we were out of

orange juice and little Wulf's dog diapers (Wulf was a cuter creature than anyone deserved to look at, with the sweetest, gentlest
heart of an angel, but he wasn't potty-trained worth a damn).
Tired, shell-shocked, and scared about our futures, Liam and I
drove to Walmart together. We grabbed the juice and then, like
two zombies, we stood staring blankly in the feminine hygiene
aisle. I remember uttering this hysterical, bizarre question,
"What kind does he use?"

And that was how it ended. Two weeks later, at the end
of February, I moved out and started a new job on the same
day. Ten days before Christmas, I'd been laid off from the job
I'd had for six years. Liam was a huge support system while
I learned how to live on my own again, even volunteering to
pay child support for the first two years after our divorce. Yup.
Child support. He would give me money for veterinary appoint-
ments, pet food, medicine, and accessories for Gunnar, Wulf,
and Pesto. I was so blessed not to have the nightmare divorce
experience of so many other women, many of which expose
actual human children to toxic separations. Liam and I were
not only civil, we remained supportive, amicable, and caring for
each other and our kids. When people ask me about one of the
things I'm proudest of in my life, it's that I chose a mate who
was able to meet me where I was at, even if it meant no longer
being together.

It was then, at forty, that my life truly began. The next
chapter was one of monumental growth and change. I grew
even stronger—mentally and physically—throwing myself
into Zumba classes, yoga, and certification as both a Zumba
instructor and a 200-hour yoga instructor. The Zumba classes
ignited a deep, passionate fire within me for life, Latin music,
and dancing. In turn, yoga taught me how to ground, tap in,

and tune in to my body, mind, and spirit. It made me a physically strong motherfucker … with love and light, of course.

As an unmarried woman, I really began to learn how to live. I had zero regrets in my life, with one exception. With all of the wild, stupid, smart, beautiful, and otherwise outrageous opportunities I've had in life, my one regret was that I didn't hold Wulf long enough when he transitioned from this world to the next, which eventually happened on a hot summer day in 2019. My one and only regret in this lifetime was that after his little soul had ascended, I didn't hold Wuflie's physical body longer. He didn't need it, but I did. So, when it was Gunnar's time to go, I lay down on top of him and held his dead body for the better part of an hour as I wailed for the loss of that brave, pure-hearted creature and his little red-headed brother, who had passed three years before him.

Now there was only one man I had to answer to: Big. Sexy. Pesto. The gray and white, once-feral, three-legged farm cat was the only guy left standing since the other fur kids had all passed away, taking an immeasurable part of my heart with them when they crossed the rainbow bridge.

Now, I'm no counselor and haven't sat down with my beloved therapist and life coach in years, so all I can do is my best to channel Dr. Todd's wisdom. Here are my uneducated musings: now more than ever, it's apparent that whatever was inside me that made me feel weird—in conventional life, in corporate America, in feeling like I'd settled for a life less than what I was destined for—had to do with my own uniqueness, my need to dream and fully explore the world and my differences.

It must have been because of that thing, which had been inside of me since childhood, that I desired to approach life wholly on my own terms and more wildly than I had once been allowed to do. It wouldn't be until forty years later, living in the jungles of Central America, that I truly became who I was supposed to be. Only then was I finally introduced to myself. She had been waiting a long time to be this free, joyful, and wild. That was when I stopped trying to tame every creature, including myself.

"LIFE IS EITHER A DARING
ADVENTURE OR NOTHING."

– Helen Keller

chapter six

NO MAP, JUST HEART

By the start of my second month in Belize, I was beginning to gain a sense of peace and belonging there. Now that I was living alone and fending for myself, I no longer had to worry about sharing a space or food with another human. If I'm honest with myself, that's a situation that really suits me well.

A few weeks after Rasta moved out of my apartment, I went on a snorkel excursion. I had to meet the boat crew and other divers at 5:30 a.m. that October morning, and apparently, they decided the south side of the island didn't need streetlights. I was glad not to be walking amongst the groves on the gravel roads, but the dark streets were eerie, which I hadn't dealt with before. Not knowing what or who might jump out at me, whether a drunk tourist or a huge land crab, had me on edge. Rasta had fixed my bike a week after it broke (once the smoke cleared a little and we tried to remain friends)—for a fee, as I knew he needed money. I jumped on my bike and headed to the village to meet the group.

As we started to cruise out to sea, I realized there was no internet connection, so I turned my phone's WiFi setting off to save the battery. The excursion was to the magical Blue Hole, the second largest barrier reef in the world. I had learned how to SCUBA dive in Mexico in the Sea of Cortez, which has beautiful water and sea life, but the Blue Hole was on a whole other level. I took in the exquisite ocean views above and below the water and the wildlife on the neighboring island of Half Moon Caye. It was amazing and peaceful.

We started back for Caye Caulker around 2:00 p.m., and when I opened my phone again to take more photos, I reengaged my internet connection. When I did, I saw that Rasta had tried calling five times and left a dozen nasty messages, saying he had come by my apartment before work that morning to grab a work shirt (he apparently still had a couple items at my apartment) and noticed my bike wasn't there. Because of this, he accused me of staying overnight at another man's house, and, of course, the messages went downhill from there. It was an irrational mess—a crazy, erratic, mean stream of consciousness.

This only reinforced his profound emotional immaturity to me, and I wanted nothing to do with it. He clearly didn't have a handle on just being friends. If I had learned one thing from Rasta's behavior on the dock a few weeks prior, it was that I had overestimated his maturity. I had assumed that, since he was older than the "bebé lion cubs" (often aged twenty-five to thirty-five) I tended to date, he'd be a rational, mature man. Apparently, just because a man had a few more years or body hairs than a dolphin-skinned youngster, it didn't mean he was automatically more thoughtful or emotionally intelligent. In fact, I've found the opposite is often true (I'll keep you posted as I continue to do more research).

We all know the dangers of making assumptions, but we don't always pay attention. Now that erratic behavior was added to the mix, I would have to pay more attention. Rasta was now predictably unpredictable. He had a mixture of personality and behavior that needed to be watched out for and treated with kid gloves. With the predictably unpredictable, there's the potential for violence.

Even after he and I had broken up, I continued to tell people we were together because I didn't want other men thinking they had a chance with me. Being a single woman in a foreign country was not what I wanted to be advertising right now. I had seen and heard of enough toxic relationships and instances of domestic violence in this tiny country that I knew by now this island wasn't where I wanted to search for a life partner or possibly even a chance hookup. Whether this was due to culture, lack of education and resources, or deeply ingrained patterns, I needed to do whatever I could to stay safe. While solo female travel is a wonderful, freeing experience that all women should have, whether they venture twenty miles or 2,000 miles away from home, presenting as having a partner was one lie I didn't mind telling. I felt it added an extra layer of protection.

I never regret giving my love to anyone because those I've loved needed that love, and I was capable of sharing it. In truth, I did still have love for Rasta, but sometimes it's necessary to love someone from a distance. I'm a firstborn, hyper-independent Capricorn woman—we are famous for our ability to draw boundaries. So, I had to draw a boundary somewhere. Typically, that boundary should be established sooner, but since I still only knew Rasta and my landlord, I had hoped he was a mature adult and could handle having a safe, stable, platonic relationship.

That night, I had dinner and a couple of drinks on the north side of the island. Before heading home for the night, I visited the bartender from the resort Mia and I had stayed at in March. I hadn't even been up there to say hello since returning to the island because saying "hello" to friends—especially men—had been such a point of contention with Rasta.

Back at the resort, I met some ladies from New York who had seen me in yoga that morning and were curious about how I ended up living there and what it was like. I told them the story in a nutshell, and they were captivated by the love story. It was one of the first times I included the detail that Rasta and I weren't together anymore. Saying it out loud was emotional, and I got teary several times.

The next morning, Rasta sent me a social media video. In the clip, a man's voice spoke to a former lover, eloquently stating that he appreciated his former partner for sharing their feelings and that he hoped they would find future happiness, even if it isn't with him. "Always follow your heart," the voice said against the background music. It was perfectly said. By the end of the video, I was in tears (again). Finally, Rasta was demonstrating a mature, adult response to our breakup and his previous childish behavior.

After Rasta sent that reel as well as some apologetic messages, we were able to communicate in a healthy way for a short while.

"I'm sorry I let you down, that was never my intention," he explained. "I will forever regret that."

I wrote back and said, "Thank you for this. It's perfect. It says it all. I only regret that we couldn't make it work. I will always love you. That will never change. And I want you to find happiness— wherever and with whoever that is." I told him I didn't want a relationship with anyone else for a very long time. Maybe in the distant future I would, but for now I would wander this world alone and find happiness in meeting new people and visiting new places. He echoed the sentiment.

For the next ten straight days and nights, it rained. The

nonstop rain turned into a self-regulated therapy session or, as I like to call it, too much time to think. Until recently, I'd lived my entire life in the rural U.S., and I always had a car. I had freedom, as flight attendants say, to "move about the cabin." Now, my livable space was confined to an island five miles long (only two of those reachable for me) and one mile wide. My world and the community I was in had shrunken smaller than I thought they could.

I lived at the far south end of Caye Caulker, and the nearest grocery store was at least half a mile away. In order to pick up even a few days' worth of food, I needed to take my bike and backpack, carrying what I could on my back and placing the excess groceries in the basket. Every few days, I struggled home with an assortment of glass bottles, cans, and veggies as I tried not to squash any light items under heavier ones. Bread always arrived looking like a ten-year-old memory foam mattress that had been found on the side of the road. And do I even need to describe the shitshow that was me trying to make it home with a plastic bag of loose eggs every week? It might not have been a water-into-wine level miracle, but it sure took some talent because where I'm from, eggs come in a carton, not a plastic bag.

So, given what a challenge even some of life's mundane tasks were, when six inches of rain covered the dirt road outside, ain't nobody goin' nowhere. I was stranded in my second-story apartment (thank goodness it wasn't ground level), wondering if the cyclones we were all closely tracking would actually hit and wash us away. Would we lose power and, therefore, connection with the outside world? We wouldn't hear any evacuation warnings if we did. Suddenly, I really regretted not buying that portable life jacket I had been considering before moving here. At the time, I thought, *geez*, that's really being over prepared. If Jesus wants you to float, you'll float, I reasoned. Of course, I didn't question my decision to pack the high-end skin care products, the stovetop coffee maker, the hidden-camera detector, the two hunting knives, the waterproof matches, or the animal-print platform sandals. Only at that stupid life jacket did I draw the line. It's like I had met with the executive producer of the TV show that is my life, and they said, "Now, do something really dumb, just to see if you make it through that."

Days into the prolonged storm, when it seemed we might have to build an ark like Noah's, I'd still had no contact with anyone except through text messages. There was no easy way to leave the shelter of my apartment, so I stayed at home and watched the downpour from the balcony hammock. Indoors, with no human contact and the deafening rain hitting the roof, loud enough that I couldn't even make a phone call or watch a movie, I just sat still. But the wheels in my mind didn't.

I thought about the noise, the rain, and how much I usually enjoy it—especially in a warm climate. However, without human interaction and the ability to go to the beach, for walks, or even to get basic necessities, I was starting to get twitchy. "Twitchy" is the word I use to describe the hours or moments leading up to a "moment," a tiny little blip in time when I am not at my best, often when I'm tired, hangry, or generally emotional about something that's probably not as big as I'm about to make it.

Not much in my life has been hindered by the fact that I'm a little twitchy once in a while. It's just the way the cookie crumbled, and it only affects my life to the extent that I let it. I don't always have a handle on the behavior as much as I'd like, but I'm good at hiding it when I want to. With people I'm closest to, though, I don't even try. They know if we're seated near children at a restaurant, I will make the hostess move us, or if someone is rattling candy wrappers or using their cell phone in a movie theater, I will march right down and tell them to quit. Those closest to me know that I am only comfortable between seventy-eight and eighty-eight degrees Fahrenheit and that I can't stand loud noises, strong scents, or bright lights. Nonetheless, I'm a pretty freaking good time, wickedly funny, and extremely empathic. I can feel someone else's energy the minute they step into a room before they even speak.

I enjoy being around people for short periods of time, then I have to recharge at home, preferably with a pettable animal. My dogs and beautiful cat were all non-licensed emotional support animals for me and never even knew it. Being around animals my whole life was probably one of the best coping mechanisms for offloading my stressful moments. My Southwestie bestie (one of my ride-or-die girlfriends in Arizona) not only has two therapy dogs but even a miniature horse named Stetson, also a certified therapy animal. But I had no such companion or outlet on Caye Caulker.

As I sat in the hammock, only able to hear and see the wall of rain falling from the sky, I thought not just about how I was feeling mentally but also physically. I didn't need constant companionship, but the island was a total ghost town, with only the rain and flooding streets for company. The days and nights of immobilizing rain were making me very lonely and uncomfortable. I thought about the drop in temperature the rain had brought and the severe increase in humidity that would follow whenever it finally came to an end. Not seeing sunlight for days and being essentially on house arrest, I was unable to even do laundry, with the washer outside and the clothesline completely drenched.

Stuck inside my apartment, I constantly looked out the

window to see how deep the water was as well as for any signs that it might let up. With each day the rainstorms continued, I said goodbye to a little more of my sanity and hello to even more of my "twitchy" feelings. Now, "twitchy" is also a term I use to describe being horny, and being trapped alone inside had me feeling a bit caliente and cachonda for sure.

The weather outside was so bad, and my apartment was so close to where Rasta worked. We seemed to be on decent terms, and I didn't see any huge issue with letting him stay the night downstairs while I was up in the master loft. We were comfortable around each other, and I knew my apartment was more quiet and comfortable than his (there I was, being an empath again). Halfway through the insanely rainy week, I let Rasta come upstairs, so we could hang out … without pants on. That did not mean I wanted to get back together with him, and I assumed he knew that too. I was just a cougar on the hunt.

When Rasta and I broke up, I had planned to head to Guatemala for two months for a change of scenery. After the culture and climate shock, the tropical illness, the new relationship, and the break-up—all in a span of eight weeks—I needed to get the fuck out of that fishbowl.

A new friend I had met while writing at the oceanfront cafe had told me she was also planning to go to Guatemala. Anna was in her thirties, very straightforward almost too blunt—and with a British accent that sometimes added to her harshness. She was also incredibly insightful, which made her interesting to chat with about many subjects. She had been to so many countries all on her own, and her travel knowledge just floored me. She was like my very own Millennial Mary Poppins.

Anna wasn't the typical lost and confused tourist. She gave off an air of absolute confidence and finely tuned decision-making skills. She knew what she was doing and where she was going. Sometimes that meant taking a nap; sometimes it meant taking a sunset cruise to watch dolphins. She swam every morning and went on tourist excursions in the evening, making the most of the Belizean leg of her trip.

We were also very different. I listened to Burna Boy, Snoop Dogg, and Romeo Santos, and she was obsessed with Taylor Swift. I discovered that my deep esoteric thoughts and dark sense of humor weren't quite "British appropriate," or maybe just not British Anna appropriate (I can't speak for the late Queen, HRM, of course). What drew me to Anna was that it was clear from the jump that she and I were both Type A, independent, get-things-done, ready-for-most-anything types of gals. She was a director of nursing, and I had been a respiratory therapist, so we traded war stories from our time working in healthcare. And, thank goodness, we were both cat people!

Anna told me that the election that was about to happen in Guatemala would potentially kick off some civil unrest and suggested we both refrain from visiting. She had been a solo female traveler for a decade and had been to all of the countries in Central America, so I trusted her. She had decided to cancel her trip to Guatemala and would spend two weeks in Costa Rica and Panama instead. I'd never been to either of those countries, and getting to explore Central America beyond Belize was very exciting to me. I asked her if I could tag along, and away we went.

Anna knew how to arrange all of our transportation needs across every country we were visiting. It would never have occurred to me that to get to Costa Rica, or Panama, for that matter, you could first catch a boat to Mexico. Anna planned our itinerary and decided the best and cheapest route would be to leave Caye Caulker by water taxi to Chetumal, Mexico, then to take a bus to Cancun. From there, we flew to San Jose, Costa Rica, to spend a couple weeks between there and Panama. It sounds crazy, but it ended up being quite logical, quick, and cheap!

We arrived in San Jose in the evening and walked through our huge Airbnb apartment building, which was one of the coolest places I'd ever stayed. The whole building had been designed and decorated in an *Alice in Wonderland* theme. It was very whimsical and next-level stunning. Anna told me she'd be going on a tour of San Jose on her own the next morning, so I wanted to find one of my own since I'd never been there before. Anna was extremely independent; we'd be in the same airplanes, buses, boats, and accommodations, but we tended to go off on our own for daily excursions. We were traveling in tandem rather than traveling together.

Without Anna, I needed an experienced guide to show me how to get around safely. I signed up for a free walking tour and hopped into an Uber at eight-thirty in the morning with a small waterproof backpack to prepare for the Costa Rica rain, which seemed like it might go from sporadic to persistent—and fast. Three minutes before the car reached my destination, I saw an email that the tour had been cancelled. In disbelief, I realized I would be totally on my own, unsure where I was in the city and with limited Spanish—which had become very apparent two days ago. I had to figure out where to go, whether this neighborhood was even safe enough to explore on my own, and if my phone's internet service would kick in while away from the apartment.

Guess what? When you're dropped into a foreign country and a limited number of humans speak your native language, it's a real game-changer. The thing is, not everyone speaks English (even we, North Americans, should know that by now). Even among the younger generations in Latin America, I was surprised to find how many people didn't speak English. It's jarring enough to try to communicate with other people when you can't find words in common, but when even ads and street signs are indecipherable? That's a "shit-fuck moment," as Tina Fey said in the cute chick flick, *Wine Country*. I had been under the impression that my beginner Spanish had progressed to intermediate, but the last seventy-two hours had me feeling dumb as shit and not even sure my English was so great. I would have to get used to apologizing to a lot of Uber drivers and store clerks for my lack of Spanish-speaking skills and my prolific use of Google Translate. What was fun was figuring out the value of the big brown monkey on blue paper versus the sloth on green paper. Costa Rican currency, colones, was bright and covered with beautiful pictures of animals. It reminded me of the group trip to Fiji ten years ago. Fijian money is so pretty that I kept some as a souvenir (or for when I return and spend it one day).

I reluctantly got out of the Uber and walked to the hotel where my walking tour had planned to meet. In a mixture of English and Spanish, the hotel concierge explained where I should walk and what might be of interest. The instructions were muddy at best, and my brain was unable to relax into my imminent solo day trip in San Jose. Right then, I realized how paralyzing it was not to feel fluent enough in a language. What would I do if I ever went to the Middle East or Asia? How had Anna traveled throughout Europe and Turkey, only speaking British English? I could read a decent amount of Spanish, but when it was coming at my ear holes at lightning speed and with different accents or dialects, my brain became a little canary whose cage was covered by a blanket: lights out.

I had two options: get into another Uber and head straight

back to the apartment, too afraid to have a go at this alone, or do my best to follow the concierge's guidance, trying not to hit a dark alley or take a wrong turn. That was how my brain worked in new, unknown scenarios—either return to baseline (the safe option) or turn the complete opposite direction and lean into fear, panic, uncertainty, and whatever perceived obstacles (real or imagined) are in my way. I chose option two and walked toward what I assumed was the city center.

After walking down the main street and some window shopping (it turned into not window shopping when I purchased two shirts), I found Cafe Rojo, which looked like my kind of place. Determined to find some cool architecture and a museum or two, I needed coffee and breakfast first, and being a coffee snob, I had to try out some unique cafes brewing the country's finest homegrown beans. The staff were so nice, and I was intrigued by their Vietnamese-Costa Rican fusion menu. The food, coffee, and service were out of this world, and I even had an impromptu Spanish lesson from a staff member named Dixon (he was patient and kind, but it confirmed that I was useless at Spanish!).

In the end, I kind of nailed my solo city excursion. I had managed to find great food and coffee as well as make a few temporary friends. Chance encounters were usually how I met and had great energy exchanges with people. And it was fun, trying to speak Spanish. My desire to become fluent was so strong, though I wasn't sure exactly why. In high school, when we chose elective languages, the cool kids chose French, whereas I was more practical and knew my life plan would more likely involve Spanish. I was right, and it was the most important thing I did in high school, besides excelling at typing and not getting pregnant. My typing skills were thanks to WordPerfect software and a very patient teacher; my lack of pregnancy was thanks to my own initiative and the Oklahoma City Planned Parenthood.

Later in the trip, Anna and I departed San Jose and headed to the jungle to tour a coffee farm and see some sloths and monkeys. After that, we headed to Panama to soak up the sun, sea, and sand again. As Anna went to Starfish Beach, I hopped on boats from one small island to an even smaller one to hang out with the freely roaming howler monkeys. One of them sat on the tabletop in front of me, playing with and biting my straw sun hat. Curious, content, and uncaged seemed like the way to be for us both.

Traveling almost by myself with Anna, and no significant other waiting for me at home, I realized how much I loved my freedom. It was something I thought I had already learned during my divorce a decade prior, and this was a reminder. I realized this was exactly how I wanted my life to be. I needed to be free—free from answering to anyone but myself.

Despite our differences, Anna and I learned from each other. In addition to teaching me how to maneuver through all of Central America, which would be crucial for my safety just weeks later, Anna also showed me the beauty of moving through life with utter confidence, despite the situation, weather, or shoe choice. Visiting Costa Rica and Panama with her changed my life forever for many reasons.

Anna is from Northern England, where they apparently speak as fast as auctioneers. I don't know if it was that British accent that gave her an edge or what. What that accent did for me, unfortunately, was make it nearly impossible for my U.S. ears to comprehend most of her words. Trying to understand her British English was like trying to understand Spanish as a non-native speaker. The only time I had an advantage was when we were sitting across from each other in a quiet cafe and I could see her mouth moving as she spoke, unless she was covering it while eating. I would normally wholeheartedly subscribe to that aspect of civilized etiquette, but in our case, I would have preferred if Anna had kept her mouth uncovered even while she was chewing a whole tomato.

We had some of our best talks over the many meals we shared while traveling in tandem. We had only known each other for a few weeks before embarking on that trip together, but we were able to converse easily. One night over dinner, we were discussing men and how dysfunctional dating was these days. Twenty years ago, a lot of men were interested in skinny blonde Barbies; now, they wanted Jennifer Lopez lookalikes. I couldn't compete with all of the curvy women who had seemingly appeared out of nowhere with asses, boobs, fake lashes, hair extensions, and fake nails. Don't get me started on the Brazilian Butt Lift (BBL!)—I didn't even *want* to compete with that. I don't see anything attractive about having a brick-shaped insertion added to your peaches, but (or should I say "butt"?) to each their own.

At one point, Anna stopped me mid-sentence, stared me in the eyes, and went Mary Poppins on me as she often did. "Your looks are the least interesting thing about you," she said with that accent and very matter-of-fact delivery. Though she was likely speaking about all females as a collective, her words seemed to be directed specifically at me. They stopped me in my tracks.

I set my fork down and said, "I'm not competing." But her comment got me thinking, which was what I needed. As long as I was my best self and happy with myself, why would I give a fuck what anyone stuffed in their butt (cheeks or otherwise) to attract a soulmate, a one-night stand, or whatever they desired? I had hoped we were all trying to be our best selves, but a lot of people seemed to put too much emphasis on their outer shell and not enough on their inner selves.

Don't get me wrong, I also post photos and videos of myself on social media because it makes me feel energized, sexy, empowered, vibrant, and alive. But how far can fake nails or some blonde highlights go in helping us deal with the deeper stuff? We also need to deal with our traumas, whether through clinical therapy, books written by experts, or even online snippets, reels, video clips—whatever the kids are calling it these days. In many ways, social media is bullshit in terms of truly healing our traumas or dysfunctions, but there's some fairly solid sound advice out there, and technology can help … as much as it hurts.

There is strength in numbers, and social media is a double-edged sword. The fake lives we see on social media only show what they want the public to see. At the same time, social media provides an outlet and a space to share our ideas and truths. We find common ground there, even as it adds to our insecurities or causes us to question our identity and whether we're "enough."

I was amazed at the number of solo female travelers I met on Caye Caulker and during my travels with Anna. Many of them were decades younger than me and had spent years traveling all over the world by themselves. I was so impressed with their independence and chill, "zero fucks" attitudes combined with their wanderlust and intense admiration for other cultures. Then, it occurred to me that I was admiring myself. For what we see in others is often a mirror, a reflection of ourselves.

I often felt like I was in some sort of wild, adventurous, survival mode, but really I was admiring the hell out of myself too, though I didn't really know it at the time. Maybe I had thrown myself into the deep end of the ocean with just a piece of driftwood while everyone else had a couple of pool noodles, an inflatable raft, and a couple of cocktail koozies, but we weren't all so different from each other. It's like the 1990s idiom, "All that, plus a bag of chips!" We have to celebrate ourselves because, let's face it: if we don't, who will? If you're not your biggest champion and hype woman, who will be? The truthful, most honest answer is that no one else will. My "mission," so to speak, was to break free of "normal"—of the average life and the status quo. While I was modestly prepared (or so I thought), I had still taken a leap, not knowing if a net would be there to catch me. That was the nature of this new journey that was developing. Once again, it was high-risk and high-reward. I had to be brave, go forth, and lead with love.

"I AM A LIONESS: NEVER WILL I
LET MY BEING BE THE BREAK ON
ANOTHER'S JOURNEY."

— Aisha al-Qurtubiyya,
translated by Yasmine Seale

chapter seven

UNCAGED

I knew when I came to Belize that it would be for five months or fifty years. That was the mantra I had repeated whenever people asked me where I was headed and for how long. I didn't know the specifics, and quite frankly, I didn't want to. The whole point of this international walkabout was to gain some perspective on my stressful, over-scheduled, urban life to slow down, reassess, and see if I could find peace and some passion in my work—my personal writing. Now, I wasn't quite sure how my writing would provide the financial support for me to subsist this way, but traveling in the tropics, writing, and dancing …. It was my trifecta, my dream life. Throw in a cat to spoil, and life doesn't get much more perfect. And if there's a good-looking, relatively emotionally available bebé lion cub unsuspectingly prowling somewhere within claws' reach? I wouldn't be mad about that either. But, regardless of how much (or little) we plan, things happen. And things were sure happening.

The evening Anna and I returned from our adventure, Rasta sent me a message that said, "Regardless of my stupid ways, I hope you enjoyed a part of the little time we spent together." I said that I did and hoped he had too. He replied, "Love and appreciate you so much. Sleep well." I thanked him for saying that, adding, "I love you too, Rasta. Sleep well." The next morning, I had another message from him. "Morning Kimberly, don't let anyone or anything spoil your day today. Have a wonderful one." I replied politely and carried on with my weekend.

On Sunday night, I fell asleep early and momentarily woke up. Checking my phone, I noticed three messages Rasta had sent and deleted, along with two missed video calls and two additional messages that said he was outside my apartment and needed a work uniform for his early morning shift. This seemed to be a bit of a pattern with Rasta, not fully moving his belongings out of my apartment. I didn't think it was him being lazy; I thought he just wanted to have this connection, or an excuse, to maintain some type of contact with me. Several times, I politely asked him to finally remove his things, but it hadn't happened yet.

Still mostly asleep, I messaged him back, and he immediately called again and said he was still outside. I got out of bed and made my way to the front door, but all I saw among the darkness outside was a sweet tabby cat who had climbed up to my second-story entrance, no doubt looking for some dinner. I sleepily fed the cat, but Rasta was still nowhere to be found, so I left his uniforms in a bag on my doorknob and messaged him saying I had done so. I asked him not to scare the cat whenever he stopped by, and then I went back to bed.

The next time I woke up—in the middle of the night, because I'm a light sleeper—there was a ton of activity on my phone. Rasta had messaged me just minutes after I fell asleep, saying nothing about his uniforms and asking if he could spend the night at my house. It was hard to sleep at his place, he complained. When I hadn't replied, his message was followed up by hundreds of calls and messages, both sent and deleted, all between the hours of 10 p.m. and 4 a.m. Literally hundreds.

I was alarmed by the scary string of one-sided communication. Rapid fire, chaotic, scrambled, illogical, accusatory, unfactual, frightening, and at a rate I'd never seen from anyone before. How was it possible for him to do so much in the span of less than six hours? The words, tone, and sentence structure were absolutely manic, going well beyond cultural differences or even toxic relationship dynamics. At this point, these radical mood swings bordered on potential mental illness.

As I lay awake shaking, I continued scrolling through Rasta's erratic array of messages, ranging from "I'm sorry to disturb you," one minute, to "You take me for a piece of shit and think you're so important. Wish I would never have to see you," the next. They only got worse and more frenetic from there, in addition to the hundreds of times he had tried to call. In terror, I recalled something Rasta had once shared with me. His brother had "a touch" of mental illness, whatever that meant. Well, placing a phone call every 60 to 120 seconds for hours on end sure fit that bill in my eyes!

In my sleepy delirium, I sent a single message, begging him to leave me alone. My reply only reignited his tirade of delusion, and the string of aggressive and inflammatory messages and calls continued. The fact that Rasta was behaving like this while knowing he was about to start a twelve-hour work shift only added to how incomprehensible and reckless he was willing to be. My body shook with the extreme stress and fear, my nervous system in absolute overdrive, unable to process what was happening. I knew I had to act, and quickly. But I would have to wait until daylight, when I knew he would be at work, so I turned off the lights and waited.

When I finally came out of my sleep haze and regained my faculties and critical thinking skills, I blocked Rasta's phone number. He would no longer be able to communicate with me, but he still knew where I lived and would come for his work clothes sooner or later. And even though Rasta probably knew better than to spook me by showing up randomly, as he was generally fearful of law enforcement, I felt safer leaving than relying on any local first responders for assistance. I had zero faith that the police would actually keep me safe (legal support for foreigners was tricky, to say the least), but I could keep the unspoken threat in my back pocket, just in case.

When I realized I had to leave, I saw two options. I could either return to the U.S. long before I had planned to return, or I could head to another country. From the time I returned to my island in Belize after visiting Costa Rica, I had a feeling I would try to go back and spend some more time in that unique and special country. I felt a connection to the land, the ocean, and the people there. So, that's where I decided to go, to a small town I had only passed through in a shuttle bus twice before, en route to Panama. Once again, I would be a complete stranger in a new country, and, unlike Belize, the official language isn't English. Would I be able to survive on my own? Was this crazy? Was I?

When you're not on your home turf, making an escape is seriously daunting. Thankfully, I now had a little community of familiar people, but I was also well aware that everyone on the island was into everyone else's business. For my safety, I had to keep what I was about to do a secret. I knew that Rasta had some days off coming up, and I had to execute my plan to get off the island before his string of work days was over on a Saturday, less than six days away. There was only one flight out of Belize City the day before the end of Rasta's work week, when he'd presumably come looking for me or might try to pull something stupid, disturbing my peace—or worse, causing me harm. To make that flight, I would have to take the water taxi to Belize City at 10 a.m. on Friday morning. From the dock in Belize City, I would take a taxi to the airport. That flight would take me to Panama City for a night, and then finally to San Jose, Costa Rica. My time with Anna had paid off.

I still had to secure housing, flights, and shuttle bus tickets, and I also had to tell my sweet landlord that she wouldn't be getting advance notice of my departure because I was fleeing the country. Not knowing the best way to tell her, I asked to come see her that day, and she agreed. When I showed her my phone records from the night before, she gasped. Fully understanding the undesired potential and gravity of the situation, Edie told me to do whatever I needed to do. I begged her desperately to tell no one of my plans. I couldn't risk Rasta finding out.

I still wasn't sure Rasta was capable of physical violence toward me, but it wasn't worth risking my safety if he ever got even more out of control. I knew Rasta had lived a hard life and ran with a hard crowd; I wouldn't stand a chance against him if it ever came to that. He'd been to prison at least once and had also stopped a swinging knife with his bare hand (apparently to save a woman's life) a few years prior. And in my mind, Rasta had nothing to lose at this point. I was no superhero (or supermodel), but I was probably the best thing to happen to him, at least recently. I gave him unconditional love, as well as some financial stability—things he hadn't experienced much of before and, sadly, might not again.

In the days leading up to my hasty departure, Edie updated me whenever she saw Rasta at the grocery store. He was usually buying alcohol and looking incredibly disheveled. She said he looked horrible, not like himself and smelling like liquor. I'd never once seen Rasta drink anything but beer and never more than two bottles. His drug of choice was weed, not alcohol.

Edie's updates only affirmed my fears, and I continued moving fast, preparing my belongings and myself for the unexpected exodus. I'd spoken with people who'd had to grab and go, taking nothing more than a backpack and the clothes they were wearing, to get to safety. While I had only moments to make a decision, luckily, I had a few days to implement it. It was better than having no days at all. If I could just stay safe where I was for the next few days, I would be free from fear and able to find peace again.

I still had a little empathy and compassion regarding Rasta's downward spiral, but that man was the reason I was fleeing the goddamn country. More than anything, I was scared for myself and in survival mode. I had put myself on that island and cohabitated with an interesting yet unpredictable creature, all of which taught me about myself and the world around me, but the fact remained that I had to leave. Immediately. All of those thoughts and more were running through my head as I tore through the two-bedroom apartment on Caye Caulker and moved my belongings downstairs. I hastily chose the small amount I would bring with me. The rest, I had to leave behind.

I had come to Caye Caulker with five bags stuffed as full as they could get. Three months later, I condensed 300 pounds of my most valuable and useful possessions into less than a hundred pounds spread between three bags: one large suitcase, one carry-on, and one backpack. You know what? It's just "stuff." In those thirty days, I had learned that only the essentials were essential, and when you travel a lot, "stuff" just weighs you down. Paring my life down to two suitcases and one backpack was freeing once I was able to let go of the perceived magnitude of what I was leaving behind. Having to choose what was most important to my survival, peace, and well-being, forced me to be brave in a way I never had been before.

At the end of the day, it wasn't brand-name yoga leggings or fancy coffee machines I needed; it was an extra-large pair of baggy cotton cargo pants, a wide array of bikinis, and a large, long-sleeved button-up shirt with a collar that protected me from the sun. It was my ten-year-old waterproof backpack, my sandals that wouldn't quit on me, and a water bottle with an internal filter that allowed me to drink from anywhere but the ocean, keeping me safe and hydrated.

Lately, I had been learning that the "stuff" that wasn't tangible was often what was really important. Like, where to find fresh produce and safe meat or which days to wash and hang laundry or what streets and neighborhoods to avoid or, when push came to shove, knowing how to escape. Every animal knows when to hunt, but they also need to know when to turn around and walk away. Every animal knows when to retreat.

I set out what I was leaving behind for Edie to disburse once I was gone. What wasn't so easy to part with were the people who had become part of my life there, who had impacted me in some way. I didn't even have time to say goodbye to them all, like the medicine man and village council member who gave me native herbs when I was recovering from that tropical illness. Then there were the bartenders who recognized me, not because I had a drinking problem but because I didn't blend in. They were so kind and friendly, especially the one who eventually made sure I was safely on the last boat I ever took out of Caye Caulker. I would miss the juice lady I had enjoyed conversations with when I stopped by every day for watermelon, soursop, cantaloupe, or tamarind juices. And, the staff at the oceanfront cafe where I did most of my writing, who gave me the "locals" price instead of the tourist price on my daily coffee and food orders. And I would especially miss Dah Root, the Rastafarian fruit vendor who liked to share his philosophy on life and love and told me green was my signature color, "like your eyes and the ocean" (I never found out if he was colorblind or if it was the marijuana speaking; but to me, my eyes and the ocean are both blue). I was so grateful for all of these people, some of whom had also told me they were glad I had come to be part of their community. Those who hadn't verbalized it had let me know in their own quirky island ways.

The next morning, Edie picked me up in her golf cart and took me on one last tour of our island. The only stop I dared to make on the way was my home away from home, the oceanfront cafe. Saying goodbye to the friends I had made there—including the bar mascot, Princess, the cat—was so difficult. On my way out, I stopped by the little cocktail bar next door to the cafe to ask the bartender for a huge favor. Though I didn't know him well, I felt I could trust him to keep my secret long enough for me to get off the island. I explained why I needed to leave so quickly and quietly, and then I asked for his help. I didn't want to be at the dock alone. He didn't ask a single question before agreeing to help me.

When Edie and I arrived at the dock the following morning with my modest luggage collection, my bartender friend (who turned out to be her cousin!) was already waiting there. He and I sat for thirty minutes waiting for the water taxi that would take me to Belize City. I felt like a sitting duck until I got safely on the boat, sad to be leaving and a bit scared that Rasta may have heard the news of my departure and could be on his way. I didn't know how he would react at that point, but I didn't want to find out. My only hope was that I could be more cunning than Rasta. If I could outsmart him, even on his home turf, I knew I would be okay.

I took a deep breath of relief when the water taxi arrived. Carrying my suitcases, I climbed on and quickly sat down, scanning the surroundings for any sign of danger. That's what prey does, and I had become prey. I typically considered myself more predator than prey; hunter, not the hunted. When I wanted or needed something, I would seek it out. Waiting for things to come to me puts me on edge, given my proactive nature and the amount of freedom I've built into my life. I sure hope, at the conclusion of this crazy story, we don't find out that I'm just a selfish fuck. I highly doubt that's where we're going, but to some, it might very well be. After all, perception is reality, and my perception, or version of reality, is not yours.

Once I had made it to the mainland and off the boat, I needed to get securely into a ground taxi without complications (or anyone recognizing me). I put my backpack on and wheeled my suitcases to the curb, where I found a driver to take me to the airport. Getting in the car, I saw a man half-sitting, half-lying on the sidewalk. His features, hair, face, bone structure—everything—were so similar to Rasta's that they could have been related. Rasta had told me these characteristics were typical in Belizeans with East Indian heritage, distinct from the Creole or Garifuna traits found in the country's other black populations of African descent. I stared at the stranger as we drove away, haunted by his expressionless eyes and gaunt face. I had seen a similar expression on Rasta many times before. I had the sense that the cultural fabric of those two men somehow overlapped in a way I would never quite understand. It was like they both shared a curse from carrying the kind of trauma that left behind scars, seen and unseen, in a part of the world where the perpetuation of violence, poverty, and corruption was higher than in my own and where resources like therapy and social services were almost nonexistent.

What I did next felt nothing short of a miracle, though it was basically just knowing how to logistically navigate multiple countries to reach a desired destination (again, Anna had contributed highly to my confidence and capability to do this). I found a hotel near the Panama City airport and spent a short night there before the early-morning flight to Costa Rica. Once in San Jose, a pre-arranged shuttle bus was already waiting to take me to my new rental home in Puerto Viejo, on the southern Caribbean side of the country. I had thought of everything, the only surprise being the extra charge for my second suitcase (I happily paid the guy 20 USD to transport me, my extra undies and bikinis, and fifteen European twentysomethings down the mountain pass.

What I pulled off took an extraordinary amount of courage and inner strength. All of that is inside me, cultivated from years of experience beyond what I've seen in this lifetime. I believe I have an old soul, one that has been around for hundreds, maybe thousands, of years. I embody the souls of warriors and goddesses and witches and ancestors and, yes, even mothers. I have always been connected to the non-human creatures that surround me for comfort, healing, and strength. All of the power supplied to me by all of those entities was what I drew from in my departure and the months that followed.

Even in prey mode, I felt the fight that was always inside of me, ready to go. While I recognized the potential for the danger I was running from, I could turn back at any moment and fight if I needed to. Sure, I was small in stature, but I was big in brains and wouldn't fight by the rules; even if there was a big chance I wouldn't win, you'd feel it nonetheless. The cougar was out of her cage. Part of me thought I'd always been out, but apparently, sometimes I was still inside, maybe with the door ajar.

There were infinite lessons in what I had experienced, and I was very much present for every one of them. Everything that happened did so as it was meant to. All the characters and colors and sights and sounds I encountered in the exact way God and the Universe wanted to reveal them to me. The challenges of life I had experienced, learning to communicate with wildly different cultures and nature itself—all of it was so eye-opening and wonderful and necessary, pushing me to the next level I was supposed to arrive at. The lessons of resilience and self-mastery during adversity were in the forefront during this semester of learning life. They're what helped me eventually put the pieces of myself back together—in a better, brighter way than before. I had to become more wild, more untamed, stripped of much of my material, Western culture-approved possessions, assumptions, and way of life, before I would realize who I was and find peace.

I might not have found that extra part of myself so quickly (or ever) if all the events of those few months in Belize hadn't unfolded as they did. My nervous system had received quite a jolt from the situation that transpired with Rasta. I could tell it was traumatically overworked, something I would spend the next six months working through.

My sense of peace returned to me almost immediately once I had left Belize and knew I was safe. Later, I would understand that I didn't leave the island because I was chasing this feeling; it was always inside of me (alongside all the little neurotic bits that also lived in there), wherever I was. Now, that feels amazing. That level of security and equanimity, though, couldn't be obtained or sustained when I felt I was in physical or emotional danger. And I was in danger on Caye Caulker. More so than I had realized.

People stay and go for different reasons, reasons that don't always make sense to us as bystanders. We find ourselves judging others' situations like Monday morning quarterbacks, telling ourselves and anyone who is listening how we might have done differently. That's easy to do when we have the gifts of time and distance, allowing us to evaluate and make potentially more sound decisions. Thankfully, I would be given the time, space, and perfect environment to recover in Costa Rica.

As I stepped onto the plane heading to another new country to discover new people, make connections, and integrate once more into a new culture and community, I hoped the inhabitants of Caye Caulker knew how much I loved them and how much they had taught me, for better or worse. I would never have come to be the person I am now had I not stepped onto that airplane in Tucson on August 14, 2023, headed for Belize.

"THERE IS NO ONE A WILDISH
WOMAN LOVES BETTER THAN A
MATE WHO CAN BE HER EQUAL."

– Clarissa Pinkola Estés

chapter eight

THE PENIS CHAPTER

Returning to an existence I'd already lived would be like stepping back into the cage and closing the door on myself. I'd already escaped; why turn around and walk straight back into my cage? That's why I moved forward rather than returning to Arizona when I chose to escape from Belize. I must have been pretty resolute in that decision because it took almost twenty-three hours and passage through three different countries to reach the Caribbean Sea in southern Costa Rica. I voluntarily took this route knowing it would be exhausting, eye-opening, and maybe even a little scary. I felt in my gut that I needed to allow the Universe to pull me in that direction. I knew I had to move forward and that that was the only route to get there.

Naturally, the lengthy travel day gave me plenty of time to reflect, gain a little clarity, and start to feel safe again. There wasn't much sleeping going on after what I'd just been through on Caye Caulker, paired with how many different boats, planes, taxis, and vans I needed to take to get to my destination. I felt immense relief to be safely off the island as well as so much gratitude for the people who had helped me along the way, including the strangers who didn't know just how much their kind gestures meant. Even a taxi driver with friendly, reassuring conversation gave me more strength to continue than he could have realized. Once I stopped doing the many "mental gymnastics" that were required to execute this escape plan and endure the long journey that followed, I sat back on the Caribe Shuttle—my final six-hour leg of the journey—and tried to relax a little. My mind was flooded with thoughts, mostly about my romantic entanglements in the ten years since my divorce and how they'd gotten me to the current moment.

We all have ideas about what love looks like and how it should and shouldn't feel. My first theory about love likely occurred to me as I was about to get married, the first time I thought I had something figured out. I had believed that relationships and marriage wouldn't work out well unless the people involved had a nearly identical definition of love. While I think there's still some merit to that theory, I've discovered there are more layers to the onion. As many have expressed before me, there are many different types of love. And all of those ideas, spoken or unspoken, are how love works for each of us. Love can't be measured the same way in all situations, and, sadly, I've come to accept the fact that love on its own is not enough to keep a relationship going. It never has been and never will be.

When I think of the word "love," I think of feeling grounded. Those who say that love gives them wings must be smoking some chronic "herbs." The kind of love I've searched for is one that feels like having a phenomenal male lead on the dance floor. He doesn't need the greatest arsenal of flashy moves; he just needs to take my hand and lead me to the floor. And when we get into our frame for whatever rhythm is playing (usually bachata, salsa, or kizomba), my whole body relaxes. I involuntarily exhale, a huge sigh leaving my body as I'm able to feel the energy, strong but calm and relaxed.

I've done some things in my years—and by things, I mean dudes. I don't like cowboy boots or country music, but I've ridden some stallions. Big, fine ones. I'm no flaky millennial or Gen Z'er, nor am I some modern, pansexual, Pisces princess. I'm just a Gen X Capricorn cougar, and we can leave marks.

My levels of wildness and tameness seem to correspond to my desire for a partner at any given moment. Now, my research hasn't been tested for scientific accuracy, but these findings may not be pure coincidence. The wilder, stronger, and braver I've become, the less I've needed a man, though sometimes I did still want one. And I didn't want a philandering, dickhead, mama's boy. I didn't want a project, a trauma bond, or a soul-contracted serpent sent by the Universe because I didn't learn my lesson the first five times. Truth be told, though, that was what I kept getting. I *hadn't* learned the lesson, so the Universe was flinging huge red-flag grenades right at my head. And each one was so pretty and seductive in his own way.

I've cried buckets of tears over several two-legged males, a couple three-legged ones, and more four-legged ones than I can count, hoping that at some point I would run out of tears. But that's not what happens, especially when you vow to lead life with an open heart.

During yoga teacher training years before, we had each been asked to create a short mantra, something that resonated within us. The phrase that came to me was: "I lead with my heart; my heart stays open." Since then, I've tried to maneuver through life that way. Doing so wasn't really hard when it came to most romantic relationships; the difficulty occurred when dealing with friendships, strangers, situations, or even family. In those dynamics, if I felt one of us (me) was making a lot more effort to foster the relationship, I released the other back into the dysfunctional wild. When I fall hard for a man, it takes longer than what I feel is healthy or acceptable to create a boundary. I recognize this, but it's hard to change the behavior.

When I adopted that heart mantra, I was in the midst of yet another heartbreak, full of angst over some dude and some penis (not belonging to the same man, mind you). You'd think I would be tired of that nonsense by now. Nope. I did it to myself, really, thanks to my heart and all of the emotions (and hormones) associated with love and lust. Hopefully, we learn before too much emotional or physical destruction (too late over here) that we are responsible for much of our own brokenheartedness. We invite new players to the team, but they bring the same bad habits with them. We all want to score, but seldom do we want to put in the long hours of training and work to make it to the relationship Super Bowl, to find satisfaction and contentment with our partners.

Geographically inconvenient and emotionally unavailable—that's how I could describe eighty percent of the situations I found myself in. I had seen the phrase on a hilarious travel-related social media post. Regarding the two men described above (well, the one man and the other's penis), one was definitely inconvenient from a geographical standpoint, and both were emotionally unavailable, masquerading as well-adjusted, healthy, highly intelligent, relatively healed humans. I'd like to put in a formal recommendation that "Dick Blindness" be added to the Diagnostic and Statistical Manual of Mental Disorders handbook. Like snow blindness, but, well, you know.

It took a really jarring experience like my situation with Rasta to wake me the fuck up. I wasn't taking subtle hints, so the Universe kicked me in the face and choked me. She kept throwing shiny, new pretty boys my way, and I had thought each time that I was getting closer to finding my person. In actuality, the Universe (crazy fucking angsty bitch) was only throwing players onto the proverbial sports field, and they were all playing with a handicap. The kicker—no pun intended—was that it was always disguised slightly differently, but in the end, it was usually the same affliction: trauma, disguised as emotional unavailability.

What makes men more challenging to love than when they exhibit their wildness? Well, as it turns out, when they can't be tamed even a little, they also can't usually provide us the comfort we need. At times, I wondered if I was just asking them to give too much of themselves away. Then I figured I should stop being preoccupied with them and focus on what was going on inside of myself. Where did my own wild and tame parts reside? The problem was, whenever I refocused on my path and remembered who the fuck I was—the powerful master of my fate—BAM, another hot guy would go and dick blind me all over again.

Dick Blindness isn't the only chronic disease with which I am afflicted. I also have a touch of BDE: Big Dick Energy. This masculine energy can be addictively strong, silent, and capable when I witness it in men. Sometimes it's necessary for us as women to manifest a little of that too. Since I'd been living on my own and making my own money, most of my decisions were created from masculine energy. I'd been a bit out of balance with my feminine energy, but I'm getting ahead of myself. I suspect my dick blindness and BDE had hindered me from seeing when men were incapable of being truly vulnerable and emotionally available. I was so distracted by the primal energetic traits I desire in men that other (maybe important) details, like emotional maturity and active listening, became secondary. Maybe some men were somewhere in between, but who has the time and emotional bandwidth to dive into a theory like that? Either you're in and available—no games—or you're out. Plain and simple. But my brain couldn't make educated decisions when it was being ganged up on by my heart and hormones.

I'm grateful for this malady, though. It was partly responsible for my less-than-traditional life and worldview. I have a single girlfriend who is overloaded with BDE, and I told her she needed to allow a little more feminine energy to flow through her. "The men worth making time for won't mind our BDE," I explained, "but no man wants it swinging at them." This applies to all of us strong, dangerous broads. We have to keep it somewhat in check, otherwise we need to shop on the other side of the store—and that ain't for me (I strictly drive a stick). I mean, unless a sugar mama wants to fund my nomad lifestyle, but I have no plans to read that how-to manual!

Some heterosexual men are attracted to strong, intelligent women who are capable and moderately independent, but straight men want and need to feel needed. They aren't looking for women with masculine energy. We don't necessarily have to invent make-believe scenarios for them to demonstrate their masculinity, but asking their input or letting them take charge once in a while biologically suits them. Can they make a dinner reservation as efficiently as we can? Probably not. Should they be planning more dates and making more dinner reservations? Absofuckinglutely. This is a difficult concept for a Type-A Capricorn who is meticulous in planning and details and timeliness. I'm very much an "if you want it done right, do it yourself" kind of girl. These are the exact traits that exude masculine energy. If I used them for exploration and self-discovery, could they help me find out who I really was and what I needed to stay balanced? Although I wanted uncaged freedom, my wildness was tempered by the need for stability and feeling grounded. I wanted loyalty, reciprocity, and safety. I wanted to be wild but tame, free but (somewhat) caged.

I had evaded discussions about it any time I sat still enough for therapy, but I had an issue with feeling safe. Always looking ahead, preparing for anything, and anticipating potential dangers was an exhausting way to live. That hypervigilance often went into overdrive with all of the adventures I've told you about (and many others you and my mother haven't heard yet!).

While the tame side of me wanted a stable, predictable mate, the wild side of me wanted, well, a wild one. It's hard to find both in a single human male (of appropriate age). How much wildness could we bring to a relationship before Animal Control personnel got out the tranquilizers and butterfly nets? A man who played by certain rules while ditching others, like I do, would be the golden ticket.

"Feminist" is probably my least favorite F word, losing by a landslide to "fuckery" (or anything else that starts and/or ends with its first four letters). That said, as I've gotten older and met other women close to my age, I've discovered that many of us are becoming aware of a vital piece of knowledge: we don't need men. Hear me out before you throw this book at me.

We don't *need* men. That means we either want them or we don't—for sex, for the occasional interesting conversation, for something heavy to be moved, for help getting a cat out of a tree. (Who are we kidding? If a cat is stuck in a tree, we're going straight to those hot fire department fellas.) In those times of want, we will notify you that your number has been selected, much like the Department of Motor Vehicles does, or—possibly a much cruder example but wildly accurate—like the New York

City deli counter does when your pound of meat is ready. The realization that this is how it works takes bravery and courage. It takes BDE.

As true as it is, it takes some of us a long time to come to the want-versus-need realization. Why? Remember: dick blindness. It's hard to think straight when a penis-owner has a pretty face and body (especially when his penis is also pretty *and* he knows how to use it). Instead of those deep-sea fishermen it showcases season after season (over twenty, apparently), *Deadliest Catch* should be about the delicious, deadly combination described above. How many times do we really want to watch guys in boats risk their lives in frigid waters just to catch some seafood? Most women could tell more entertaining "deadliest catch" stories of their own. They're almost guaranteed to be even more harrowing than Daryll and Buck bobbing for snow crabs.

For all of the points I'm trying to make, I can't just change what moves my heart, soul, or vagina. I had broken free, and, just like the genie doesn't want to go back in the bottle, this cougar wasn't going back in her cage. I wanted an evolved animal: a man with the loyalty of the alpha wolf, who mates for life, has the heart of a lion and strong pride based on a matriarchal lineage. The male lion protects his pride at all costs, but the lioness hunts, leads, helps make decisions, and raises the cubs. Ignore that last one: you know I'm not raising anyone's cubs. The closest I'll get are those delicious entanglements with younger men.

This lineup of "the world's elite," also known as "the small population of men I've shared a bed with," could be described as an origin story of sorts, a small encapsulation of my overall narrative that has shaped a significant part of my life and evolution. As much as I wanted someone who could be thoughtful, kind, and reserved, I also wanted someone to be my champion and my cheerleader. When shit hits the fan, I need you to protect me with your life. I realized that much of the reason why I was attracted to certain men, outwardly and inwardly, was because they had either a high degree of wildness (nature) or were trained to be that way (nurture) or both. This wild streak often puts them in prison, on the streets, or in the military. In the case of a couple of my favorites, they checked more than one of those boxes.

My awareness of who I actually was to become and what I wanted for myself began at age forty. It was then that I felt an awakening, becoming alive to all things on an all-new level. With earphones in to drown out the other passengers and the eighties rock music blaring in the shuttle, we bounded down the Costa Rican highway out of San Jose and headed south toward Panama. I thought about James, my ex-husband's fellow skydiving friend. He was the domino who tipped over all the others.

I vaguely remember the first time I met James. He was very tall, very gorgeous, and muscular, with dark skin and a huge smile. He always seemed happy, like he was loving every moment he was living. Similar to Liam, nothing was too challenging for him. James was a pilot, a West Point grad, former military-turned-successful, director-level professional and nationally awarded skydiver. Both he and Liam were great, extremely capable humans, but they were different people with different energy. James had swagger—in spades. Spades and spades and spades. And he didn't even have to try. In fact, James was almost dorky, but he was so hot and sweet that his dorky sweetness only added even more swagger. When he kissed, I would later learn, there was no trace of dorkiness. It was all swagger and powerful, sensual energy, like there was no one else on earth but the two of you.

From the beginning, James has been one of those people

who is good at keeping up with, and checking in on, those he cares for. He's the type to sporadically reach out or pay a sudden visit to his friends. One day, a couple months after my divorce, he called to check in on me. James was shocked to hear about what had happened, but he was supportive of both me and Liam. We were all friends and knew that would never change. The bond that we and our other skydiver friends had was an unshakeable, friends-for-a-lifetime type of bond. We talked about how long it had been since seeing each other eight years ago and how I needed to get away, to travel on my own as a newly single woman making her way back out into the world.

I was planning to fly to California early that autumn for a trip with two other friends. We had planned to visit wine country, near where James lived, but my friends backed out at the last minute. The solo trip that resulted was probably infinitely more fun because I was reunited with James instead. We cruised around to various vineyards, drank wine, and enjoyed the breathtaking Sonoma County views over fresh oysters. It was perfect.

Even before I knew I would be staying with James that trip, I packed new undies, not wanting to wander around our Airbnb rental in something that wasn't cute. That turned out to be the right call because James was shown them and way more, and I was shown hidden portals to new dimensions and other worlds and galaxies. Well, that's a slightly dramatic way to illustrate how my body and brain went into complete sensory overload when James and I kissed ... and stuff.

As good as it was, it was also confusing. I had been married to one of his best friends (I mean, was that *supposed* to happen?) and was in complete shock that this gorgeous human wanted to kiss me. Yet it also felt expected in a way. I don't know. Perhaps there had been some signs that I, for whatever reason, hadn't paid much attention to (Reasons like: I was married!). For example, one summer, long before the divorce, James came to visit us. Liam was working at the motorcycle shop he owned with another one of our skydiving friends, so it was up to me to entertain our guest. Lucky for me, we lived in one of Arizona's only towns with a body of water, and our friend had a beautiful speedboat she invited us out on for the day. So, we grabbed a bottle of booze and off we went.

At some point while we were on the water, our friend was taking photos, and James and I squeezed together tight. As we posed for that photo, I felt something—something big (not literally, ladies). Maybe it was the combination of slightly wet skin, Mojave Desert sun, 110-degree heat, and a little alcohol, but it hit me in the chest, and I felt a liquid, magnetic energy pulsating throughout my body for a brief moment. As our skin touched, my back inadvertently arched a little, out of shock and other things I couldn't or wouldn't understand at the time. I wouldn't understand until fifteen years later in Sonoma County, California.

When we finally joined together, it was like my soul left my body. It felt as though time nearly stopped, along with the rotation of the planet itself. If the Earth spins around its axis at around 1,000 miles per hour, we had entered a twenty-five-mile-per-hour zone. When I came out of that trance, hours had gone by. I was still in shock, but I realized something: I had always loved James and had had *no* idea or refused to put those pieces together. That's just self-preservation. Maybe we had a cosmic, karmic connection that was never supposed to be denied. It was quite the gift, a unique gift that felt otherworldly, untimely, or from another timeline entirely, from lifetimes ago. My mere human condition would spend years pondering it and trying to find it in other men.

But James had a free, wild nature in him. He was the type of perpetual bachelor heartthrob that couldn't be pinned down, sexy in a George Clooney (or, more appropriately in this case, Idris Elba) way. He could never be mine, no matter how badly I wanted him to be. Every day for the next five years, it would rip me apart at the seams emotionally and mentally. During that time, James and I would meet up on occasion, and each time we did, I hoped it would be the time he would finally tell me he loved and wanted only me, that I was enough for him.

Once I finally came to terms with the reality that I would never hear those words from him, he flew to Arizona and said exactly that. He turned to me as we were hugging after I picked him up from the airport and said, "It's time." I didn't even know what he was saying because I had completely accepted the fact that he would never be able to offer me that. I had no idea what he meant. "Time for what?" I asked. He replied, "For us. You and me. Let's do this." Well, fuck me sideways. (And he did).

The relationship lasted four months. Our old patterns and traumas wouldn't let us find peace, and we had to let go. Nobody enters a relationship as a perfectly healed, fully evolved grown-up without trauma. But sometimes, even the best of us hit a stalemate. We can commit to work on ourselves, whether with a professional, through loads of self-help books, or over brunch with enlightened friends who've already done therapy, but we can't move forward with a partially healed human if they don't want to move through (and past) what's haunting them. I have my own demons haunting me that I convene with every day, but I won't hold congress for anyone else's. We have to find a way to slay our own dragons while walking each other home.

Never underestimate a modern relationship's ability to mystify, horrify, or disappoint. We have moved past "simpler times" and into the age of polyamorous relationships and phone swiping to see where what nearby hot guy is DTF (down to fuck) or which of the many men these days think they're enough to satisfy their wife, girlfriend, and side chick all at once, while keeping them a secret from each other. Let me throw in a rule we ladies have tried to teach ourselves in theory but fall short of in practice: *manage your expectations*. We get our hopes up that some thing (or person) will be so spectacular when it often isn't.

Relationships are all-consuming and captivating in the beginning. They are exciting, enthralling, exhilarating, erotic, enlightening—all the great words that start with "e," allowing us to almost completely forget our existence before they started. That bewitching time in between beginning and breaking point is a delicious distraction, full of newness and joy and chemistry and lots of sex. Then, we find ourselves at the inevitable conclusion, where those "expectations" probably weren't met and "e" comes to stand for ending or evaluating (as in your life choices) or episode (as in the credits rolling after an episode of *Cops* or *Real Housewives of New York City* or *Deadliest Catch*—you see where I'm going).

In the five years after my California reunion with James, I had been consumed by it, and having to admit we weren't going to end up together after so many years of yearning and hoping left me heartbroken almost beyond repair. I was emotionally, mentally, and physically exhausted, and it was a major factor that had sent me to Belize the first time. In the years between our first impactful encounter and our attempt to make a relationship work, I think I subconsciously hoped to find him somewhere in each new lover and relationship. At times, I found bits and pieces of him, but it was never enough. I couldn't find his unique essence or someone who could love me like I felt he did.

In the end, though, he hadn't loved me like I needed him to after all, which meant that I in turn couldn't be what he needed. I don't blame James or harbor bad feelings toward him for anything. He was the origin of an amazing journey. My experience with him made me realize I no longer carried certain fears I'd held for a very long time. I was no longer afraid of a plane crash or an angry ex-husband coming after me (though thankfully that was never part of my story) because I had gotten to experience the surreal physical and metaphysical expression of love with a human who oozes love out of every pore of his body, and he gifted that to me. It was a feeling of completeness different from anything I'd experienced before. Our story was like a love letter I never wanted to lose. That kind of love was stronger than fear. But I have always wondered, did he love himself as much as he loved me? If he did, would we have found a way to stay together?

It took two years, several brief but passionate love affairs, and a move abroad to start distancing myself from the emotional fallout. We'd had to say goodbye as lovers and partners, and I allowed our situation to take me down. Still, James and I remain the closest of friends to this day, and I cherish him more than ever. Thanks be to all the gods and all the heavens above, we are great at that.

Our relationship also explained what attracted me to strong and wild men, whom I associate with the ability to keep me safe. If they love me, I assume they'll protect me at all costs. If they don't, then that's not love to me. I want a tough, intelligent, quiet type who is barely able to express his feelings for me, but when he does, it's because he's overcome with emotion, driven by his undying, everlasting love for me. It's undeniable, and he lets me know with a subtle, sexy gesture that renders me speechless (as if) and makes my clothes fall off.

James affected my taste in men, including the energy, physical appearance, and especially swagger that I was drawn to. If I met someone with swagger that felt remotely close to his, I wanted to ride that train till the wheels fell off. Sometimes that meant dreadlocked hair, a foreign accent, beautiful dark skin, noticeable tattoos, piercings, and sometimes questionable pasts were par for the course with many of these hot male life lessons. The cultures and nationalities would change, but they were the same *type* of man. My pattern was apparent even to my friends, some of whom told me I needed to change my taste in men. This wasn't new to me, but it was completely off base. I had zero interest in boring or tame.

There are many lessons and experiences that have greatly impacted my views and choices. So many choices from my past I wouldn't make now, and I'm sure that process will continue as I follow my path of life. I really like how Brett Larkin puts it: "The Wild Woman archetype embodies the untamed spirit of feminine power, characterized by intuitive, primal instincts and unbridled authenticity." I would move through different stages of "wild" throughout my life, but I had no idea how much wilder I'd get the *older* I got.

"THE WOMEN WHOM I LOVE AND ADMIRE FOR THEIR STRENGTH AND GRACE DID NOT GET THAT WAY BECAUSE SHIT WORKED OUT. THEY GOT THAT WAY BECAUSE SHIT WENT WRONG, AND THEY HANDLED IT. THEY HANDLED IT IN A THOUSAND DIFFERENT WAYS ON A THOUSAND DIFFERENT DAYS, BUT THEY HANDLED IT. THOSE WOMEN ARE MY SUPERHEROES."

– Elizabeth Gilbert

chapter nine

NO MAN, NO PLAN,
NO PROBLEM

Does a wild animal break free from its cage only to stop hunting or exploring? No. Neither did I. I was scared, but my desire to roam free of my own volition was greater. After what I had just gone through in Belize, I knew I needed a peaceful environment to regroup, gather myself, and figure out the next few steps. I had to push past all fear to get to the other side.

I was hopeful my time in Puerto Viejo, Costa Rica, would be just what I needed, but I had to get through two more weeks of chaos first. At this point, I felt I required quite little: running water, a toilet that flushed, and not needing to run from dangerous humans. The water didn't even have to be warm (which was good because it wasn't!). But I had rented a nightmare of a house, with plumbing that didn't want to cooperate and a gas tank-powered stove top that promised to take off at least my right eyebrow. Despite learning to be more flexible and adjusting to any situation on the fly since moving abroad, I still needed a certain semblance of calm in my living space.

I fought with the rental company to get a refund and, by the second week, had already found a new place to live. I wouldn't battle like a Viking for my housing refund because I was done fighting. I was tired, and I knew at an elemental level that peace was already inside of me. And then I found external peace—ironically, with Vikings.

Casa Vikingo, Spanish for "Viking House," was in the jungle a couple miles north of Puerto Viejo, 300 meters from Playa Negra (Black Beach). It was owned and run by Erika, a female "Viking" from Norway. On arrival, I was greeted by her and her large, equally friendly dog, Cuatro. Erika was kind, attentive, and a real no-nonsense badass. I could tell she would make sure the whole property was operating as she saw fit. With the help of Erika's very capable groundsman and jack-of-all-trades, Armin, Casa Vikingo was by far my favorite place I'd ever lived.

Puerto Viejo turned out to be a dream. It's known for being in an area of dangerous ocean currents and plenty of surfing. A lot of tourists and expats come through and settle there, so the town has built itself up to accommodate the tastes of the many different cultures that occupy it. There were a number of restaurants serving up delicious food, local tico (Costa Rican) food and many other types and nationalities. I'd learned that in any of the countries I traveled to or lived in, I could never go wrong with an Italian restaurant (globally delicious!). There were also several health food and wellness shops, so finding items like chia seeds and essential oils was no longer fruitless, like it had been in Belize.

There were numerous cute resorts, hostels, and hotels in and surrounding the town and many talented local artists who lived there—not because they were necessarily Costa Rican, but because they called Puerto Viejo home like I now did. The tropical weather was amazing, and the water of the Caribbean Sea was comfortable even on a hot sunny day, which most were. The sporadic downpours came in biblical proportions, pouring quantities of water that brought the plants to life and made the jungle seem like some giant lung, slowly inhaling and exhaling as it absorbed nourishment.

As for the jungle I had the pleasure of inhabiting, I'd never experienced anything like it. As a child living on a farm more remote and removed from town than my new jungle was, or surrounded by neon blue water on tiny Caye Caulker, nothing could have prepared me for living in this part of the world. Every day, I felt a sense of awe and a deeper connection to nature than I'd ever experienced before. The different flora and fauna brought more joy than I'd ever known. I was filled with gratitude every morning, looking out the window to see the tropical trees and leaves, the sounds of birds and howler monkeys roaring in the background.

The first time I heard the noise outside my house, I thought it was a very loud kennel of dogs barking that someone was intermittently opening and closing the door to. It would come and go, get softer or more intense. The roar was astounding. Because this property was close enough to the mountains west of town, the vocalizations of the monkeys were thunderous and sounded like they were just a few feet away. I would soon learn they could be as far as three miles away and still sound like that. For six months straight, I heard them almost every morning and afternoon. The vibration of their sound alone calmed me in a way that was magical and powerful. I am dying to hear them again.

Oddly, I always feel more at home when I cook my first pasta meal in a new kitchen. Before that, I usually seek three things after landing in a tropical spot: a papaya, a jar of local honey, and a couple cans of tuna. Papaya is incredibly nourishing for so many reasons, and I love it for all of them, especially that the seeds (when ingested as directed by your health care practitioner, not me) can prevent and treat certain parasites. Something like that. Either way, it seems like a very smart and delicious thing to eat when you are living in foreign places and are concerned about unwanted tenants in your stomach. Local honey is full of immune boosters and nutrients, and when added to lemon and hot water, it is the most comforting drink there is (don't tell coffee I said that). Lastly, I'm not sure about you, but I can open tins of seafood—tuna, oysters, octopus—and just eat it out of the can. Quick protein that doesn't need refrigeration. I've even flown with them, but most of the time the TSA *really* deliberates before deciding whether a particular can is safe to go for an in-cabin airplane ride. If there's even a teaspoon of extra liquid in it, it's a no-go.

The other reason for the tuna is the ability to share it with stray cats. Those wily, skinny little stalkers are enchanting (and a little scary) when hungry, and there is an overabundance of them in Central America. I had no idea I could love stray street cats as much as my precious man, Pesto, but I photographed hundreds and said hi to every single one. When someone wants to see pictures of my journeys, every fifth image is probably a cat doing cat things.

As I got settled into Casa Vikingo, I noticed some small bowls outside, presumably for feeding animals. Erika explained they were for a cat who showed up frequently but inconsistently because he was leery of the dog—and people. The very next morning, the cat showed up before anyone but me was awake! He was a gorgeous tabby tomcat with a glorious black and gray ringed tail, just as Erika had described him. Mo—the name they gave him—was lemur on the bottom, but that head was all tomcat, with a round, strong neck and the thick "tomcat cheeks" they use in fights. Male cats apparently grow them when they aren't neutered early in life. My darling Pesto has those tomcat cheeks too.

Mo was shy in the sense that he wasn't sure of me, but he was sure enough to inquire about his chances of getting an early meal. Lucky for him, I had just been to the store and bought one can of tuna: stray-girl/stray-cat protocol. He wasn't a fully feral cat and was clearly used to being fed by humans, even coming close enough for pets as I opened the tuna suspended in oil, and split it with him. Mo cleaned his plate and then we sat on my floor to get to know each other (with the front door open—I wasn't about to trap a wild, stray cat in my house!). Like Pesto, Mo and I didn't meet until well into adulthood, so we had to figure each other out.

And just like that, I fell in love with another guy. This time, his eyes were golden green and framed by hair in shades of brown and black, scattered with some gray. The next morning, I told Erika that Mo had made an appearance and how much I would love seeing him every day. (I also disclosed that he may be wandering around with diarrhea after his oily dinner but that, at least, it was delicious going in. Plus, he was a stray cat; he'd eaten worse.) Erika was delighted—about our interaction, not the potential diarrhea—and stressed that Mo didn't really go near any other humans. A short while later, Armin handed me a small bag of cat kibble, and I noticed he had also put two clean bowls under my patio table.

Early the next morning, I peered sleepily through the large glass doors, and there was Mo! He was sitting quietly and patiently by his fresh bowls, hinting that he wanted some crunchies. I walked out, and filled his bowl.

Well, this was a great turn of events! Just days before, I had been living in a very busy tourist town with plumbing that may or may not work at any given moment. Now, I was a five-minute walk from a quiet beach of pristine black sand. I was in an aesthetically pleasing space, with lush tropical grounds, a pool, a hammock, and the perfect relationship: a gorgeous male cat who came and went as he pleased but cozied up to me once or twice a day when he wanted a meal and his ears scratched. We'd have a brief conversation, he'd bite one of my ankles, and then we'd hug goodbye until next time. It sounded a little toxic, but it worked for both of us. And at least he was pretty consistent: breakfast and dinner. True to form for a spoiled, domestic pet, he seemed to know how to tell time and even showed up early for his meals, just like Pesto.

I learned quickly where Mo's wild-versus-tame threshold was. Thanks to him and Madre Tierra's healing embrace, I also learned mine in Costa Rica. Just like Mo, if you overstimulate a human or other creatures, they might retreat, bite, or freeze. The old soul in this body of mine, my astrological sign, and my hyper-independent nature (paired with the nurture I'd received) all contributed to my levels of wild and tame.

Most of us humans respond like Mo if we feel smothered or scared—and, conversely, also when we're under-nurtured. While I am completely over blaming everything on our childhoods, some of these behaviors do, in fact, stem from how we perceive we were raised (and, remember, perception is reality). My perception of my reality was that I had been overly coddled by one parent and emotionally neglected by the other. Similarly, when cats are overstimulated, they "act out," maybe pounce. If they're feeling bitchy, they pounce. It's why most people like dogs. A dog is rarely ever going to think, "Man, I'm getting too many belly strokes; let me bite this lady." After reading that laundry list of "cattitudes," I've become even more convinced that I am a feline.

In my new life in Puerto Viejo, I pushed a wheelbarrow to the store each week to return home with a five-gallon bottle of water, un bidón, and walked one and a half kilometers each way to get groceries, even if it was just a couple of cans of tuna for humans and cats. There was also a small gourmet market 300 meters from my house, but a single orange costs $6 USD there. I knew from living on Caye Caulker that anything imported was very expensive due to the logistics of transport, and oranges fell under that category. It was sometimes hard to find food that would fit into my budget, and though I still got some things at the gourmet market, I never bought oranges there!

"Hunting" for food, being woken by the beautiful sounds of howler monkeys, trying not to step on poisonous dart frogs while walking barefoot, and a host of other amazing things that are unique to the jungle (and rainforests) contributed to my feral-ness. When I wanted amazing produce at really inexpensive prices, I had to walk into town on Saturdays to visit the market, la fería, located in a big community-run building near the center of Puerto Viejo. If I didn't leave before 7:30 a.m., all of the good produce and homemade goods would be sold out. So, even after late-night dancing on Fridays, it was early to rise on Saturdays. I was starting to grow adept at life in my new home and hoped that however my future played out, it would allow me to stay in this wild and magical place for a while.

As I'd expected by now, life in this part of the world came with some unique problems (first-world *and* third-world) that I hadn't necessarily dealt with until my move abroad. Add them all up, and you get one result: Feral. For instance, let's not forget that I was trying to speak a language I wasn't as good at as I liked to think. Searching for words, I sometimes felt like a toddler about to throw a tantrum because she hadn't yet learned the words to communicate or like an animal that could only bite or bark to express what it wants. Feral.

If that wasn't enough, did I mention the plumbing? In much of Central America, toilets aren't able to flush paper, so bathrooms have trash cans for *used* toilet paper to go into. And the plumbing issues didn't end there. One time, I had to wash all of my clothing at once in a huge bathtub because the one washer all sixteen guests shared was broken. Let me tell you, the quickest way to turn fifteen pounds of clothing into fifty is to dunk it under water in a full-sized whirlpool tub. I had to clumsily wring the water out by hand before running downstairs to the backyard before the items dripped everywhere, where I would hang them on the clothesline. It took four days to dry my clothes.

Equally, life was much more "tranquila." I cooked most of my own meals, did yoga on the beach, and took loads of photos and videos of the wildlife that showed up right outside my door. I developed an obsession for birds—not just bird*watching* but also listening. In rural Costa Rica, the tropical birds sang at least twelve hours each day. I installed an app that recognized their songs, identifying what species I was hearing based on the sounds they made. All I had to do was sit in the kitchen or outside the door, and it picked up the sounds of unique and colorful birds like parrots, toucans, hummingbirds, and numerous flycatchers.

Beyond the edge of the waves and the powerful, grounding, soft, volcanic earth was a jungle, complete with all its inhabitants. I went there every day for a stroll or some sun and watched the sloths as they tried to find suitable tree-hugging positions. One day, I told the sweet, three-toed creature not to make me come up and rescue him. He was dangling by his arms over fifty feet up in what looked like a precarious manner, but it was probably just how he spent a regular Thursday afternoon. Thank goodness because the likelihood I was getting on a ladder to assist him was slim to none.

I became enchanted with most of the other local animals too: frogs, snakes, coatimundis—all of the creatures, really. No matter the location of my temporary homes, I sought out animals. I needed to see nature, both in the form of wildlife and domestic pets. One-sided conversations with the animals in the trees were completely normal to me. I may have been the only one communicating with words, but standing with another living being like that is a form of communication, an energy exchange. Each living creature shares its energy frequency and vibration with others, no matter if they're savage or subdued.

Being a surrogate cat mother to Mo, the stray, took up a considerable amount of my time because I let it. I lived for it, really. He got two meals a day (sometimes three because he wouldn't shut up) and a little saucer of oat milk afterwards. I'd estimate Mo started spending sixty to seventy percent of his time with me (inside the house!). This was partly because I spent much of my time writing, cooking, and relaxing in my sweet space on the gorgeous property, often leaving only for some beach time or exercise.

Whereas Pesto had been feral when I met him, Mo was just wild. Pesto wanted to be tamed. Mo, on the other hand, gave up some of his wild just to be with me. It was like how I had given up some of my wild (okay, most of it) to try and live a traditional Western life. He went on nightly jungle prowls to hunt for food, but it didn't stop him from begging for meals (and I guarantee my house wasn't the only place he was getting them from). I think that cat had a circuit. He must have strolled through all of the jungle resorts around Playa Negra, gathering snacks everywhere he went.

As much as I saved Mo, he saved me. I loved him in such a different way than Pesto. I knew I wouldn't be in Puerto Viejo forever, and I prayed fervently that whoever would feed him after me would also give him some extra love. Maybe he would forget me, and that was alright as long as he remained content and healthy. As for me, I would forever be in love with my little tigrillo gatito, the king of the jungle. El amor de mi vida.

Southern Costa Rica has a completely different landscape than most others I had experienced, and I'd witnessed some truly spectacular sights in my very fortunate lifetime. Up close, the different textures and tones of the land and jungle cast magical spells, but none like the jungle-fringed black sand beach. Playa Negra's sand is very black—hence its name—somewhere between the color of graphite and hematite, with golden flecks that glimmered brilliantly when the sun was shining. The ebony sand and strong riptides swirled the clear water, giving it iridescence like my favorite gemstone, labradorite. Maybe that was part of what was so alluring to me about the environment.

One morning, as I walked and heard the loud waves warning of the riptide, the sound pulled me in, begging me to come closer. The water's appearance was extremely calming, flashing blues, greens, and purples as it picked up the sand. At once dark and crystalline, the waves lapped onto the soft black shore. Oddly, I was reminded of pencil lead. I had never seen a beach like it. It was hard to process the exquisite beauty all around (and I'm not overselling its magic—I promise!).

Once in a while, I would meet an acquaintance in town for a meal or a live performance at a local bar, and Sundays were for the best fucking Caribbean buffalo chicken wings. I ate these things like chickens were running out of wings. Whenever I showed up on Sundays, the waiters knew what I was after:

half-price margaritas and "alitas de búfalo." What's more, the restaurant was on the black sand beach, just a five-minute walk from my jungle casita.

I found healing in the jungles and Caribbean waters of Costa Rica, and if I could, I would do it exactly the same way, over and over again. I would want to get right where I was, with all of the knowledge, stories, and war wounds. It was the best eight months of my life.

There wasn't a chance I could stay away, now that I had witnessed this stunning natural beauty. So, to my soul sisters who are lucky enough to go on a final trip to spread my ashes (hopefully no time soon): our destination has changed, ladies. They were supposed to go into the oceans off the eastern coasts of Fiji and Belize, but we'll need to amend that last will and testament. Of all the places I'd been in my almost forty-eight years, the only place I wanted to be was in the Limón province in Costa Rica on the Caribbean Sea.

"I SOON REALIZED THAT NO
JOURNEY CARRIES ONE FAR
UNLESS, AS IT EXTENDS INTO
THE WORLD AROUND US, IT
GOES AN EQUAL DISTANCE INTO
THE WORLD WITHIN."

– Lillian Smith

chapter ten

EVERYWHERE AND NOWHERE

That January, for my birthday, I didn't wish upon a star. I wished upon the moon and a tree of monkeys. Two days before the full Wolf Moon, I headed north along the beach on my usual late afternoon walking route. A couple of women and a child were staring at something up in the trees. "Es un perezoso?" I asked. They said there was no sloth, but there were some "congos," howler monkeys. They watched for a few more seconds and then walked away, but I couldn't move from that spot for what felt like forever.

With my back facing the beach and the incredibly loud waves, I stood transfixed, watching the troop of howlers above me. There were even a couple of babies following the adults up and down the branches. It only got more spellbinding as they started their trademark chanting, that deep, guttural, powerful roar. I listened and watched and wished that I could hear live howler monkeys every single day as I had for months now. I was in the right place at the right time, which seems to happen a lot—with the exception of the presence of the beach flasher. He must have thought what I wanted for my birthday was to see an overweight man emerge from the jungle with his shorts around his knees.

I had already received every single immediate wish I had made between Christmas and my mid-January birthday, and honestly, I didn't think I should make any more wishes. Granted, two of my wishes were just for Mo to be healthy and safe and that he would show up for Christmas Day and my birthday— which he did! But then there was my wish to stay in Costa Rica for longer than my initial return home date would have allowed, and that also came true. Now, that was really something. It was more than coincidence; it was divine intervention. All the same, I was feeling insanely blessed.

One of the most important lessons I'd learned so far in this part of the world was that there had to be a natural flow to things. I had been well familiar with the concept, but I hadn't been utilizing it to the fullest. I started trying to implement it more in my life rather than just articulating it by sharing a funny meme on social media. I came to truly accept that what was meant for me would inevitably come to fruition. All the rest would (and sometimes wouldn't) teach a lesson, fun or otherwise. Think about W. W. Jacobs' *The Monkey's Paw*, where the characters keep wishing for situations they desire, and it yields horrific results. In other words, good comes with bad. Always. That theory, combined with my track record, is why I no longer manifested or asked the Universe to drop the perfect man on me. While fun and captivating for a short while, what "landed" on me in the past now needed to stay away.

It was a powerful week. All cats aside, I meditated and pondered during the full moon, two days after wishing on the monkeys. I sent out intentions for guidance on ways to stay in this corner of the jungle near the ocean. I asked for abundance, enough to comfortably support all my needs and responsibilities. I mean, I did need money for more than just feeding two cats and a small but very hungry human. While deep in prayer, I didn't receive any specific directive from the cosmos, so I knew I needed to try a little "go with the flow," combined with a "you're still a responsible, full-grown adult."

The main reason I had to return to the U.S. was Pesto, the three-legged wonder cat I had shared my house with for the better part of ten years. He was mostly worth it: as wonderful as Mo but in different ways. My two loves were very different creatures, but one thing was for certain—they would kill each other if they lived in the same house. Mo had a home here in Central America, and Pesto would continue to live out his days stress-free in North America.

I was trying to flow more in all areas of my life, and I applied the practice to all the nouns: persons, places, and things. I would not fight to keep someone or something in my life that was not aligned with my highest good. For those that wanted out, the door was right there. This trip wasn't meant to put me in Central America for the rest of my life; I had to return to the U.S., regroup, and allow another plan to cultivate in a way that was exciting and aligned. I hoped that meant remaining peaceful and happy while I worked on writing projects and figured out how to jump on the next plane for another travel adventure.

I wholly believe in the Maya Angelou quote that explains she believes we aren't free until we accept that we belong everywhere and nowhere. She said, "You only are free when you realize you belong no place—you belong every place—no place at all. The price is high. The reward is great." I'm willing to carry that thought even further: I firmly believe we're all made up of the fiber of where we've come from and where we've been. Our individual fabric is made of the places of our ancestors. I am North American by nationality but Lebanese, German, English,

Irish, Dutch, and French by bloodline. Through my travels, I was now also infused with Mexican, Spanish, Fijian, Belizean, Panamanian, and Costa Rican influences. Each place gets into our fabric if we're open enough to receive this gift. My fabric was strongly influenced by both North and Central America, and I knew I wasn't done in Costa Rica. I felt that deeply. I had an attachment to the land, but I was open to discovering so many more places.

Traveling isn't just about the place; it's also about the people, the culture, la energía, and vibes. The magnetic pull of Costa Rica was stronger than anything I'd ever felt before. I felt the land, the plants, and the animals speaking to me, asking me to stay as much as I was asking the same. I don't think this happens very often, a point in life when not only do you want to be in a certain place but the place wants you to be there too.

Many of us travel not just because of wanderlust but because we knew that where we began wasn't where we were supposed to end up. I'd been called to these places I had no claim to, possibly because, from childhood into adulthood, I looked around so many times and thought to myself, "This doesn't feel right." But how do you quantify what that means, especially as a child? That gypsy blood had always been in me. It came from my mom— believe it or not, the same sweet little lady who had aspired to be perfectly content as a wife and mother. I could feel her wild nature beneath, and after my parents' divorce, I saw her travel more freely and on her own. As different as she and I were, we had a couple similarities, after all.

Compared to many people, I'd been to a lot of places; compared to others, I'd barely scratched the surface of the globe. I thought back on the times I frequently switched locations and what I did to feel more grounded and settled when I did. Some of these places I visited were home for three days; some, for three months. Some were large inland cities, and others were very small islands. Certain places had me wishing I could live there (most of those happened to involve warm weather and the ocean). But, ultimately, they were trips—with a beginning, a middle, and an end. I always had to return home, out of some obligation or another. Even if my time in Central America had a sort of "choose your own adventure" conclusion, I would eventually leave—about nine months after arriving.

We can't predict human nature—or any nature, for that matter. I'd heard stories of people who had come here with big dreams and even bigger bags of money, only to be spit out by the land itself. To me, though, there was something incredibly maternal about the land and energy in Costa Rica. Most days, as I wandered among that nature, I felt an unexplained presence in the air around me. It always carried the same message: "Don't go; you need to stay. You're safe here." As someone who doesn't feel safe in most places, that message was powerful. I'd been living there for less than two months, but I was already feeling healed in all the ways—of heartbreak, grief, and lingering intolerances for myself and others. It was ironic: the place I felt safest was the wildest place I'd ever been.

I could feel the land granting me safe passage. I knew it had no ill intentions, including the time when a ground bee stung the underside of my foot. I was walking along the beach and had no idea he was meditating there and that I was about to step on his head—until he shoved his ass knife into the arch of my foot. I apologized to him, then promptly pulled out the stinger as the pain set in. Poor guy. I'd sting someone if they were stepping on me too. That day, I learned a new sentence in Spanish: "Una abeja me picó la planta del pie."

One morning, shortly after my birthday, I had to get up early for a photoshoot. I try to do one each year to celebrate the strength and beauty of aging and to capture images of new perspectives in unique locations. I had met a local photographer, who started by taking some pictures of me on the black sand beach. As we moved around trying different backgrounds, we moved into the jungle beyond the sand. To get through the thick jungle trees, I had to traverse a carpet of vines, heart-shaped leaves, and roots that protruded from the ground.

The photographer asked, "Are you okay with taking your sandals off?" He could tell I didn't fully understand what he meant, so he continued, "I think it's always best to ask Madre Tierra for permission to safely come through." Now I understood. I had followed a barefoot guide through the rainforest in Fiji, but the jungles here were a different story. This was home to some very dangerous creatures. As tiny as they are, a native viper's bite could end your life.

I removed my sandals and silently asked that I be allowed to safely tread barefoot, thanking Madre Tierra, Madre Selva, and Madre Mar—Mother Earth, Mother Jungle, and Mother Sea— for their strength, healing power, and blessings. As I begged for protection from poisonous creatures while pretending to be a supermodel in the jungle, I thought about a recent discussion with a friend, who told me something like, "What you find beauty in is really what you see in yourself." Later, I realized she was probably paraphrasing Rumi, who said, "The beauty you see in me is a reflection of you." Probably.

Regardless, in Costa Rica, I found beauty everywhere and in everything (though not necessarily every*one*). I hoped my new rose-colored lenses would follow me everywhere I went, even if I had to be far from the jungle or ocean. Though I knew by now that I didn't want to look at many more rocks or cacti, the desert landscape I had left behind for Belize.

Between the vivid colors of the waves on the beach, the birds, and the sun in the sky, beauty was reflected back to me constantly. If there was any truth to that Rumi quote, I must have found myself stunning. And, yes, I did—but I also knew that my looks were the least interesting thing about me. At the same time, I saw how aging was changing me. I was starting to show mental age (lower tolerance for human nonsense) and physical age (lower collagen and titties). Ladies, in case no one has told you yet, lather that sunscreen on your face, neck, and hands. Our necks age faster than our faces! Knowing that, I was almost tempted to wear a scarf around my neck at all times. And my legs were still cute, but they weren't as awesome as they used to be. Those quadriceps could stop traffic six years ago. Shit, they were hot, and I appreciated them, but would I have appreciated them even more had I known how tiny they'd get? Possibly. I didn't have as much juicy muscle in them or my glutes anymore, but I was still going to cruise the beach in the tiniest of bikinis. I didn't give enough of a shit to cover up. Those cheeks need to feel an ocean breeze.

The tropical jungles, rainforests, and Caribbean Sea agreed with me. They had brought my whole being to life—heart, soul, and all the rest. That humidity bestowed a dewy glow that took at least ten years off of me. Of course, behind that dewy glow was an oppressive heat that brought sweat to places you wouldn't think possible, but my skin had never looked better. On a wildly superficial note, I'd never had so many people come up to say how much they admired my style (apparently it was "a vibe"). I only had a small amount of clothing and several swimsuits with me, but I mixed and matched them every day to keep cool and absorb some sunshine, but not too much. After all, most of my ancestors weren't exactly meant to live this close to the equator.

Once I journeyed to Central America, I had found my version of paradise in an actual place. There was something incredibly moving about the sloths slowly and purposefully stretching from one tree branch to another, the overhead monkeys, the poisonous little frogs and lizards, colorful birds, and so many hundreds of other species. They weren't all friendly either, so while contending with some crazy and, at times, life-threatening weather, there were also dangerous, life-threatening creatures. Cute, but deadly.

Most notably, during my time in Costa Rica, I felt absolutely wild. The energy and vibration of the jungle and its inhabitants felt aligned with mine, and that in and of itself was calming. I was grateful for who I was and how far I'd come. I may have gotten skinnier, but I was no less feisty, and I was surely not the scariest thing touting flesh on the beach (some men—of any age and shape—love to wear tight, tiny swim trunks).

Traveling—with all its variables, unknowns, and unfamiliarities—really forced me to come to grips with my HSP tendencies. You may recall that HSPs need structure, order, and a controlled environment to avoid overstimulation. But, in order to accomplish a goal, communicate in a foreign language, or just find some moments of peace, I had to work through what I was feeling without spinning out. And, funnily enough, you know where I wasn't overstimulated? The Central American jungle. It was like the wilder the natural environment around me was, the calmer my internal environment felt. None of the chaos or frenetic energy that usually aggravated me existed in the jungle. Every day, I awoke to alarming monkey roars and heard the cackling macaws and mealy parrots screaming overhead, but none of it fazed me.

A conversation with a woman I met in Costa Rica, another

Brit, brought about an epiphany. Like me, she felt very connected to Costa Rica and loved living there. She explained that it felt as though she'd lived many different lifetimes in Costa Rica. I understood what she meant. I believe in past lives and previous lifetimes, that the soul in my current body wasn't "born" in 1976. It had been around for centuries—possibly millennia—having experiences through other places and timelines. The soul in this tiny cougar body had seen some shit.

Prior to my current existence, might I have belonged or existed in this part of the world? Maybe that was why I felt so at home and at peace there. That could explain why the last year of travel had had such a profound effect on me. Or maybe I had just eaten one too many of my jungle friend's chocolate marijuana edibles and thought I could also swing from the trees! In today's society, we have to be concerned with appropriating other cultures. How does that play into this feeling that my perceived home was never really my home? Where does one draw that line? That line was incredibly blurred to me because I believe people should be allowed to travel where their hearts call them and love who their hearts choose.

I thought about glorious Madre Tierra (Mother Earth) in that part of the world. For me and my sweet friend, Costa Rica carried a vastly different energy and was wildly less tame than where we had grown up, in London and rural Wisconsin. We had both removed ourselves from our familiar habitats, and—like coal becomes diamonds and sand becomes pearls—we found that a little pressure induced growth.

If you allowed it to, the potential for personal growth came in powerful surges, like waves on the beach. I had experienced plenty of internal deep dives. Sometimes, they took me down deep, and sometimes they were just a gentle nudge. Usually, they took me in the direction I needed to go. It wasn't an accident that I was born and raised in a place that felt strange to me. I believe everything happens in our lives that is meant to—no coincidences—in order to push us further toward who we are meant to become.

Regardless of why or how, there were specific factors in that part of the world that seemed to occasion personal trans-formation—and fast. Whether it had to do with the land, the weather, the elements, or the creatures, everything there came in accelerated form. Nature's magic was undeniably in your face, amped up, and in vivid, living color. With all of the sun, rain, and humidity, perhaps humans, too, could grow and change as fast as the flora of that tropical climate. Rapid growth seemed to be the key theme all around.

That conversation helped me connect the dots between the immense changes I had undergone and think back to the idea of belonging (everywhere and nowhere). I'd spent months trying to articulate the enchantment of Costa Rica and what living there had done for, and to, me. While I hadn't seen any literal births or deaths in my time there (there were plenty of metaphorical ones), a lot of "life stuff"—the sandwich fixin's in the middle—got some really good scrutiny. The truth was that I had learned more about myself and life in my year in Central America than I had in the forty-seven years prior. This journey had taken me as far north as the Yucatan and as far south as northern Panama, but there was something in the energy and vibration of Costa Rica that specifically captivated me and allowed me to grow, expand, and heal. The growth and evolution and change I had experienced in my short time abroad made me wonder how much more there might be to discover about myself and the world around me.

As much as the year had been the most beautiful, transformational experience I'd ever had, it was also the starkest overhaul of my life. I believe everything that happens in our lives pushes us further toward who we are meant to evolve into. The kids these days call it a "glow up," when we seek personal development to be the best versions of ourselves. *Progress, ladies and gentlemen, not perfection.*

Life was hard in these foreign countries, for sure, but I had never been happier. Once I broke free of Western culture and its concrete jungle to live more primitively, I felt so incredibly rooted and grounded. And most living things need to be rooted in order to thrive. I connected so deeply to the land in Costa Rica, whether I was walking in the jungle or standing in the ocean. I even felt grounded just walking down the streets of that small town.

And I was far from alone. I met many people who came every year for a month or two to escape the cold, some of whom had even bought a house there for that purpose. When I asked them why they had chosen southern Costa Rica, the answers varied, but all of us had one thing in common: we were magnetically pulled to this place.

I greatly appreciated whatever it was that served the beautiful purpose of grounding me in calmness, stability, and safety. I knew that was no one's responsibility but mine, but certain places and people made it more attainable. Knowing that, I would one day follow my yellow brick road back to the jungle and the sea because my heart told me to. Glow, baby, glow.

"MAYBE THE PAST IS LIKE AN
ANCHOR HOLDING US BACK.
MAYBE YOU HAVE TO LET GO OF
WHO YOU WERE TO BECOME
WHO YOU WILL BE."

– *Candace Bushnell*

chapter eleven

THE SAIL AND THE ANCHOR

I returned to Tucson on a Thursday afternoon in April. I guess that made it springtime in the desert. In Central America, every season felt the same, ranging from hot to hotter and rainy to rainier. The seasons were marked by what seafood was available, not the color of the leaves on the trees. Being that close to the equator, everything was always gloriously green.

I went right home and started downsizing immediately, throwing away or donating any item in my possession that wasn't absolutely vital or didn't bring me joy. I thought I had done this the previous year when I got rid of so much before moving to Belize. But, after being away for so long, I was stifled by how much stuff I still had. I had been living out of two to three suitcases for eight months, and that's what I wanted to continue doing. If I hadn't needed these things then, did I really need them now? I decided I didn't, with the exception of the important papers, a couple mementos, the items in my tiny fireproof safe, and, of course, Pesto.

Pesto was the most important thing in the house. When I arrived after being gone for a year, this sexy male cat of mine didn't punish me for leaving him. Instead, he demanded a snack as I walked through the door, and then we proceeded to lie in bed together for the better part of twenty-four hours. His love, "cattitude," and feline energy were the only things I needed. That, and a few bags of groceries delivered to my door, a modern convenience I missed.

As I cleaned, reorganized, and rid myself of things, I planned on repacking my carry-on with items I knew I would actually need for future travel. I was already thinking about where to travel next for a longer term. The thought of staying in one place, especially one I had lived in for ten years, was strangling me. Not being able to wander where I pleased made my chest feel tight.

Back in the U.S., the abundance of conveniences actually made me a little uncomfortable. I had gotten used to walking two to five miles a day, but my friends back home offered to pick me up for nearby gatherings. I had to tell them that if something was within two miles of me, I would walk. If it was farther, I could jump in their car at the two-mile mark. It was ninety degrees with no ocean breeze, so the opposite of cooling and refreshing, but I noticed how restless and unsettled I felt without my daily miles on foot. It seemed the feral and free nature I had adopted wasn't going to change any time soon.

Reuniting with these friends, I got a lot of questions. Everyone in the U.S. seemed to agree that I had come back "changed." Luckily, most of them affirmed I had become a better version of myself and were very curious about what I was up to next (apparently, no one had time to read my blog, or many of their queries would have already been answered). I was happy my loved ones were interested in my journey, but there wasn't much point in trying to fully describe what I had gone through. It was all such a different lifestyle and mindset than what most of them had ever known, and I knew very few of them would get it. The people in my support circle didn't understand how it felt to try to communicate, read signs, find safe water, navigate transportation—anything really—when common language is taken away. They had never had to maneuver through a hurried crisis situation in a foreign language, like in the Panama City airport security line when I didn't know the Spanish words for, "Fine, I'll remove my belt, but my pants will slide down to my ankles." (Never travel in thong underwear unless you're prepared for your butt cheeks to be seen. You just never know!).

So, to prevent breaking their brains, I usually offered a simplified description of my year abroad. Doing so took some deep digging and a lot of improvisation, like the kind you need to book an emergency escape plan involving travel through three countries and three modes of transportation. It was yet another layer of resilience I hadn't possessed before this walkabout.

Tucson is a relatively big city, full of traffic and busy roads, but it was quiet inside my little house. Back in the city, I found I enjoyed staying home most of all, where it was peaceful, comfortable, and I had a cat. What else could I need? The first week I was back, the mornings and evenings were very chilly, so I set my heater to kick in every time the house temperature fell below seventy-five. Then, the following weeks warmed up, but I didn't even notice when the temperature inside reached ninety degrees. I was so used to the high heat and humidity that it no longer fazed me. Aside from a couple of ceiling fans spinning on low, I still used blankets and sheets in bed to stay cozy.

The dry, urban desert surroundings of Arizona made me feel a little disoriented—similar, I imagined, to those poor, skinny, wild coyotes that roamed down the residential streets in the middle of Tucson. I felt uncivilized when I left the jungle for the big city of San Jose, Costa Rica, and again upon reentry to the

U.S., where I tried to buy a Starbucks coffee with "a monkey and a shark" because I had no U.S. currency.

Not everyone I reunited with was a fan of the version of me who had returned to Western culture. A close friend of mine confessed she wasn't sure she could "handle me" anymore. My wild had been trying to emerge for years, so our relationship had already been a little strained, and she couldn't process this new, changed me. Hearing that the most joyful, impactful, and transformative year of my life was something a loved one wished had never happened was as infuriating as it was painful.

Spiritual leader Ram Dass once said, "We're all just walking each other home." Those of us who are brave and daring enough to fight for more will inevitably leave behind those we've outgrown. As we level up and move on from our old existence, we lose some people we thought would be in our corner forever. It can be a painful and confusing part of the journey, but eventually, we learn that not everyone can walk us home.

The thing is, we often don't know we're traditional or normal or weird until we meet someone who's different. As enlightened and evolved as some become, many still remain tame—by choice or force—and a struggle can occur when we don't want to remain as others want us to. My wild was hard for people who preferred to fall into a traditional, mainstream way of life. We either have to appreciate each other for our differences or go our separate ways.

One night, Mia and I were catching up on the phone, and she asked how I was doing. I tried to explain how life felt weird and different since leaving the jungle and returning to the desert, traffic, and the fast-paced city. I mentioned that even getting behind the wheel of a car now made me very anxious. She countered, "This is where you came from, and you're the same person.

How could life possibly feel so different?" *No, girl,* I thought. *You are the same.* You could take the girl out of the jungle, but you'll never take the jungle out of the girl. Quite frankly, I hoped I wasn't the same. I always knew I was different and would want different things than "normal" people might.

I was reminded of my brother, who had an exquisite brain that never turned off. As a child, he talked endlessly about whatever specific topic fascinated him at the given moment. Depending on his age and which phase he was in, that might have meant trains, dinosaurs, army generals, Native American tribes—you name it. The kid was a real history buff and loved to draw pictures, read books, and engage in conversations about these topics with anyone he thought could answer his questions. In actuality, he was wildly more intelligent than his peers, and he wanted to know as much as he could about these subjects of interest.

Because of this, he was considered an odd kid. He may have had a touch of ADHD as a child (and possibly a touch of bipolarity as an adult). The point being: life, as it were, was hard for him. He was different, so it was always harder for him to fit in and find his way. It was a bit like how life became for me, post-jungle experience. Sadly, I never got to see Joey thrive or mature, as he died of an accidental heroin overdose two weeks before my thirtieth birthday. He was twenty-eight.

Like Joey, my only sibling, I was fixated on something: my time in Central America. I'd come to call it "my time in the jungle," or "jungle life," which probably made me sound a little like Tarzan or something. That is actually what I felt like, though: like I had crawled out of the jungle and now had to figure out how to live in "normal" society again. When someone tried to entertain me with their latest life updates at a very civilized brunch, I'd be thinking in my head, "That's *nothing* compared to living in the jungle." But we all have our version of "jungle." For so many in the Western world, their equivalent of the jungle might mean Starbucks running out of almond milk or Uber Eats not offering their favorite restaurant for delivery. I get it: perception is reality.

In June 2024, I had been back for exactly three months. Enough time had passed to affirm some things and birth new awakenings. I sent a message to Edie to see how she was doing on Caye Caulker. I was a little scared she might have tragic news about Rasta, but I missed her and my little apartment and wanted to check in.

She said she was doing fine, and we messaged for a bit, and then she asked if Rasta had found me. I told her he had called me on Christmas Day from a Belizean phone number I didn't recognize. He quickly wished me Merry Christmas and apologized for how he had behaved. I said I understood but that I was hanging up and would be blocking that phone number too. I hadn't heard from him since. Edie proceeded to tell me he had since gotten back together with his ex-girlfriend, the drug addict. Apparently, she hadn't changed and was still strung out and cheating on him. Edie went on to say that it was a sad situation and that Rasta had beat her in the middle of the street—the street that ran between my house and his. He had beaten her so badly that she was in the hospital awaiting surgery. I didn't need any further confirmation that I had done the right thing by leaving the island when I did. My gut knew I had to leave. Thankfully, I had listened to that instinct, and, sadly, I was right. That could have been me in the hospital, or worse.

Truthfully, I was shocked to hear that Rasta had gotten so violent. I started shaking even as Edie and I were still communicating back and forth about it. While Rasta's messages to me had been frenetic and very scary, he had never threatened physical violence against me. I knew he was physically strong enough to do so, but I just didn't believe it was in his nature. However, an odd and uncomfortable moment came to mind.

One evening on our trip to mainland Belize, Rasta came out of the shower with a towel wrapped around his waist. We were joking about something in the kitchen when the towel fell off his body. Then, he walked over, grabbed my arm, and started slapping me with his dick. At first, it seemed totally harmless and even funny—believe me, ninety-nine percent of the time, I love a dick hitting me anywhere. After a minute, though, I was done. While his penis wasn't quite as big as a baseball bat, it did have some weight to it, and I tried to jerk my arm away from him to get him to stop. But he wouldn't let go and just kept slapping my legs with his dick. I started feeling trapped and panicked, realizing just how much stronger he was than I was. Finally, he stopped, but situations like that sometimes end very badly; fists or actual weapons are used and do real and devastating harm. I know for other women (including Rasta's ex-girlfriend), they have.

Women often fall for a pretty face (or penis) if we see potential in a partner, but the truth is, we should never settle. We can't ignore the red flags and settle for the bare minimum of what we desire or for the potential we think we see in a man. Just because we see something in another human doesn't mean they're ready to see it in themselves; they may never. I had an idea of what life with Rasta would look like, and I truly didn't think I was asking for much. When I was honest with myself, I saw that I was lowering my requirements based on the expectations I had placed on him and the potential I'd seen in—and for—him. That, and the fact that he had a pretty face (and penis).

Believe it or not, it took those three months to overcome the culture shock of returning to my home country. Some parts of me were still very much of Western North American culture, like my affinity for hot water and throwing used toilet paper into the toilet, but the new Central American parts of me needed time to integrate. I had to adjust to a vastly different climate and secure a new job—another work-from-home corporate America job—after being unemployed for almost a year while I was away. But I also wanted to get away again. The new me was already a better, more well-rounded human, and I knew I needed to develop these recent awakenings further. I started considering my next adventure.

How could I already be thinking about moving again? The answer fully came to fruition during a visit with an acquaintance from my local group of magical, intuitive friends, whom I lovingly referred to as "las brujas." We were less about casting spells and stirring cauldrons and more about a shared belief in the supernatural power of things we cannot see. Many people consider that "faith." After all, turning water into wine is definitely supernatural, and it also requires some mastery of chemistry and elements. Tucson had a lot of us brujas, or witches, and we tended to recognize the type pretty easily. When we did, a bond was often quickly formed.

That's how my relationship with Britta developed. She worked at my favorite metaphysical shop, and we energetically vibrated on a similar frequency, even though our approaches to life and mysticism were different. When I saw her after my trip, she echoed the feedback I had been getting from all of my friends: "What do you mean, you're feral *now?*"

Most people had a little smile on their face when they pointed this out, but they were all earnest. They had always thought I was a little feral, and they had loved and cherished me for years. Those were the folks I would keep close to me, the ones who loved me wild. After all, at some point, one of them might need to shoot a tranquilizer dart at me if I continued to travel to untamed places.

Britta and I dove into the quirkiness factor of my personality, and she asked whether I had any next moves or goals. I knew I wanted to head somewhere for a longer term, but I also knew by now that working and living in another country can be a logistical nightmare. Taking that into consideration, I'd set my sights on a new location that wouldn't necessarily remove me from "corporate America." After all, money doesn't grow on trees, not even the stunning, lush behemoths that keep the monkeys and sloths safe.

Britta told me she was born in Tucson and had lived there all her life, with no desire to move anywhere else. For her, even vacationing was highly stressful, and she preferred to stay at home, where everything was familiar and comfortable. By contrast, the main theme of my year abroad had been the opposite of "comfortable," including a few threads of unpredictability, excitement, surprise, fear, and wildly over-the-moon joyfulness. I would take those feelings any day, even if they came with discomfort or grief. I wasn't made for a constant stream of comfort. I'd known for a long time that that would never be me, and my friend—this sweet, insightful little homebody—broke it down for me in one phrase. She said, "You are the sail, not the anchor."

Britta was proud of and amazed by me for going and doing all of these things I wanted to do, moving anywhere I wanted to be. Not everyone, including myself, stopped to think about the bravery, courage, and sense of adventure it took to do what

I had done so far. It was nice to hear it expressed, especially by someone who didn't want that for herself.

Her words completely threw my assumptions about my place in the world on its ear. I didn't need to fight the part that couldn't be anchored but needed to feel grounded. I had exploring to do, and that lifestyle requires a lot of sailing, going with the flow, and only once in a while stopping to drop an anchor.

For years, I'd needed to recharge after social gatherings at home, preferably by hugging a pet (or five). Anxious? Squeeze that chihuahua. Sad? Kiss that three-legged cat's head until the pain stops. Walking along the beach or on a jungle path was the quickest way for me to feel centered and grounded. Ironically, I had to get on an airplane (the opposite of feeling centered and grounded) in order to have those adventures I needed. Life balance, I guess.

I missed everything about my life in Costa Rica: the people, the places, the animals, the tropical environment. So, exactly one year after deciding to move to an island in the Caribbean, I chose my next adventure: Puerto Rico. Same tropical region, different country. In a perfect world, I would pack up my North American cat and my two Central American suitcases and head right back to where I had just come from, but it was more complicated than that. Still, it felt inevitable that I would end up somewhere nearby.

But what if it wasn't actually that complicated? What if I'd found a way to sidestep the roadblocks that might keep me from living my Caribbean dreams? Let's face it, after what I'd already done, I felt like a force to be reckoned with. What if I could do, or be, anything?

So, there I went again. In less than three months (no wonder I was confused and tired), I would be pushing the envelope by heading back to Caribbean island life. This time, just as much was at stake: my livelihood and safety in the great unknown, another completely foreign place. Maybe even more so this time.

But I could live with that. I *had* to because the genie couldn't be put back in the bottle. What I had set in motion when I stepped onto that airplane from the U.S. to Belize for a second time couldn't be undone. There was no turning back, and why should there be? Why progress forward along this beautiful journey of discovery only to turn backwards? The same feeling from the year before had returned inside me. Something in my life was telling me it was time to move on, that there was so much waiting for me if I could just be brave enough to leap. And there was. So, this cougar brushed aside her cowardly lion (think, Wizard of Oz lion, not African jungle lion) fears and jumped.

I prepared to leave on the same day I had the year before because it felt like the karmic, cosmically aligned thing to do. On August 14, I would visit my new island for a week of discovery. Two months later, I was tentatively scheduled to relocate there because a job opportunity that allowed me to work from Puerto Rico presented itself, as if it were meant to be. I had found a way to live in the Caribbean while staying gainfully employed and working on my book. Flow, baby, flow!

In the movie *Evan Almighty*, Morgan Freeman's character asks, "If someone prays for patience, you think God gives them patience? Or does he give them the opportunity to be patient?" While these lines didn't save the movie at the box office, I find merit in them. The sentiment came to fruition for me while I was living abroad. I learned to be much more patient, moving according to a vastly different schedule than that of Western culture. Absolutely nothing operated when, where, or how you might think it would (or should). This caused me frustration at first, but then it melted into patience. It was also an opportunity to ask myself if what I didn't like in others might actually remind me of my own behavior. Were they mirroring something I saw in myself? Yikes, Rumi's philosophy strikes again.

My meaningful travels were also an opportunity to develop courage in spades. It was courage that allowed me to undertake the huge task of redesigning my life in the first place, not just last year but each time I've done so. And just like the cowardly lion, I continued forward on my journey in the face of fear. Echoing the words of numerous historical figures, "Courage isn't the absence of fear, but acting despite it." I'm so grateful for my courage and bravery, but there was always room for more.

Morgan Freeman's character continues on to ask, "If someone prayed for the family to be closer, do you think God zaps them with warm fuzzy feelings, or does he give them opportunities to love each other?" Well, my travels had also created a beautiful way for me to connect with my family. My mom had raised us with an exhaustive—and exhausting—laundry list of warnings. Had I ever followed it, I'd never have gotten where I was. Instead, I carved my own path, and my mom was insanely supportive and encouraging of all of my adventures. She sent supportive girl-power texts at random moments (they usually included Taylor Swift lyrics citing female empowerment and strength). Mom's favorite concept was that we should all be whoever we want to be. As Mom (and Taylor) says, "haters gonna hate." Mom was right. I could do and be whatever I wanted to, no matter what anyone said, following my heart and making connections with creatures all across the globe. I could be my own sail.

Even still, when we try new things, they don't always work out the way we had planned or hoped. So fucking what? At least you could say that you'd done the thing, learned the lessons, gotten the t-shirt—as well as maybe the most beautiful sunset of your life or the best damn conversation or the most epic kiss (or dick) you'd ever known. Did that really look like failure in the end? If so, ask yourself, to whom—someone outside of yourself, projecting their opinions onto you? The last I checked, this is my game, I'm the MVP, and the rest of y'all are either cheerleaders on my team or on another squad entirely.

Following my heart and pushing past my comfort zone begged me to continue listening to myself and allowing my wildness to roam. In *Women Who Run With the Wolves: Myths and Stories of the Wild Woman Archetype*, Dr. Clarissa Pinkola Estés digs deep into the instinctual nature of women, how we've suppressed it for so long and how to reconnect with it by becoming the wild woman. In a nutshell, the wild woman is a powerful, magical creature who has tapped into her inherent inner strength and primal nature. This type of woman is a challenger, opinionated and unafraid to be her authentic self. But she may have suppressed this part of herself, only to finally reclaim and embrace her true nature so she can find freedom and ultimately peace. As women, we can live a "normal" existence for forty (or sixty) years but know there's more out there for us, whether that means clawing our way out of a dangerous situation or merely needing a break from domestic life.

I am a woman who runs with wildish domestic cats rather than actual wolves, but the concept and feeling still apply. When I stepped on the plane to Belize, and then to Panama and Costa Rica, I was walking away from "normal" life. Now, the challenge was keeping that wild balanced—being wild enough to live a beautiful life and be my authentic self but not so wild that I would say, "Hold your shitty mustard" to the fast-food worker (yes, that happened). I'm not proud or happy about it, but sometimes the wild overcorrects and ventures into the shadow side, also known as "asshole territory."

When we become imbalanced, we can manifest anger, chaos, anxiety, or fear of not being in control. In me, that often means my masculine energy takes over. Dr. Estés suggests that we can counteract this imbalance by first acknowledging that we have this wild side and then trying to understand it. We then need to turn toward the green space, Mother Earth, spending time in nature to pacify our untamed side—the side that needs to feel wilder. We can embrace ceremonies or rituals that connect us to nature, practices that also connect us to our inner strength. I had done that by living in places where nature provided a constant stream of awesome beauty while displaying overwhelming power. Respecting the dangerous currents of the oceans; asking permission from Mother Earth before stepping into the jungle; living amongst the howler monkeys, sloths, poisonous frogs, and vipers—these were ceremonious and ritualistic themselves. It couldn't get much more wild than that. Llevó la selva en mi corazón: I carried the jungle in my heart.

There are many beautiful words to describe the wild woman archetype: creative, instinctual, natural, untamed, spirited, uncaged, courageous, powerful, intuitive, independent, free. Many times in life, having my wild so close to the surface has been my saving grace. I strive to embody those traits while staying balanced and strong in my feminine energy. I'd been called a "warrior" by a friend, a "guerrera" by one of my lion cubs (he was trying to say "soldier" in English), and "Indiana Jones" by an Uber driver. As I prepared to embark on my next adventure, I prayed with all I had that I was built of the kind of magic, strength, and resilience others saw in me.

"I SEE MY PATH, BUT I DON'T KNOW WHERE IT LEADS. NOT KNOWING WHERE I'M GOING IS WHAT INSPIRES ME TO TRAVEL IT."

– *Rosalia de Castro*

chapter twelve

ADAPTACIÓN

No one is more sensitive to their physical location than we HSPs, and Costa Rica was the location I had come to think of as "home." Mi corazón y mi alma están en el Caribe. And at this point in my journey, the only way to move back to the Caribbean was to take a job with a company located in Puerto Rico. So, I let go of my rental home and once again got rid of my belongings. I left Pesto, the three-legged wonder stud, with a dear friend and split everything I owned among four suitcases and a backpack to fly to my new island home.

While beautiful, island life had so many challenges, one of them being weather that's more dangerous than landlocked living. Trying to feel grounded on an island is hard for a girl like me (I might be the sail, but I still wanted to feel anchored most of the time), and I was still grieving the loss of my previous life in Costa Rica. I mean, if you loved your life and missed your loved ones and the beautiful existence you once had, wouldn't you do everything in your power to get back there? Well, Puerto Rico was as close to Costa Rica as I could get.

That said, Puerto Rico is not Costa Rica, and I never expected it to be, though I had hoped they would be more similar. In Costa Rica, I had peacefully lived in a tiny casita in the jungle, and my time was all my own since I wasn't working a job. Puerto Rico was overwhelming, and I worked a stressful, full-time corporate America job in the large, loud, crowded city of San Juan. There were so many variables between the two; in fact, the main commonality between them was that they were both in the Caribbean.

The first eight weeks in Puerto Rico felt similar to my time in Belize, though there was the added language barrier that was reminiscent of my time in Costa Rica—but more intense. Costa Rica, of course, was a Spanish-speaking country, but on the southern Caribbean side, there were lots of tourists and expats, so I could get away with being lazy with my Spanish skills. In Puerto Rico, though, the majority of all situations I found myself in required that I use my mangled Spanish to convey my needs.

It would be an understatement to say I was overwhelmed on a few occasions (and cried out of frustration in the back of at least two Uber rides per week). I didn't regret the move for one second, but my existence there was nothing like it had been 1,500 miles south. I was in the Caribbean, where I'd told myself I wanted to be, but I was completely alone again. My short time in the Costa Rican jungle had made me feel completely at home. While being away from the jungle came with certain minor conveniences, it was mostly just painful. Taking a wild woman out of the jungle and placing her in the big city ... well, it felt unnatural.

In Puerto Rico, I didn't feel like I was blending in at all. In fact, it was almost more obvious there who was from the island and who was a tourist. Sometimes, it was even noticeable—from how people looked, spoke, dressed, and even walked—when those native to Puerto Rico hadn't lived on the island their whole lives.

I was desperate to blend in and didn't want to be viewed

as an outsider, so I got pretty good at noticing certain details. Observing the locals, I saw many examples of what balanced feminine energy looked like. It spoke differently, moved differently, and dressed differently. I envied it. Those embodying more of their feminine energy looked less anxious and more at ease, effortlessly beautiful in accepting their outward appearance, whatever it may be. I didn't only witness that in women but in men too. They took so much pride in their appearance, showing up and showing out, even if just at a colmado, or a dive bar, for a few beers. And I guarantee you—everyone was wearing their best cologne! Their signature scents were like calling cards, and anytime I hugged someone, I'd be reminded of them until I showered again.

Puerto Ricans seemed to have an effortless and elevated style about them. The curves, skin tones, and varieties of wavy or curly hair and hairstyles were lovely to observe. These people are stunning, unique from each other in many ways while still somehow unified in their appearances. The confidence they exuded was next level. No matter if someone was short or tall, overweight or skinny, they wore whatever clothing they wanted to with confidence that showed in their movements, especially when dancing (which, in Puerto Rico, could occur any time and anywhere).

I admired these qualities I was witnessing, but I couldn't fully embody them, not while I was alone on a foreign island with no support system. Without help from others, I felt I had to be strong all the time to fight for my survival. No matter what humans or Mother Nature threw at me, it was up to me to stay alert and prepared. These facets of my personality required masculine energy, and I was exhausted from feeling this way. Trying to prove I was worthy of being on the island and being accepted by its people was a constant battle. It was draining, mentally and emotionally.

On top of everything, a rather bizarre phenomenon occurred while living in San Juan. Every morning for months, I woke up not knowing where I was. It took me at least twenty seconds to reorient and "locate" myself again. In the meantime, I would lie there and listen to the ambient noises outside of my beautiful apartment—roosters crowing, reggaeton playing in the distance, birds squawking like pterodactyls, humans yelling and singing, gunshots going off, car engines sounding, and so on—and wonder, *Where the fuck am I?* Every day, like a real *Groundhog Day* situation, I woke up with a sense of alarm and anxiety.

Not once in Belize or Costa Rica had I woken up not knowing where I was. Even those first few days before I knew the deep, guttural bark-like roars were howler monkeys, I always knew I was sleeping in a jungle. Part of me thought that my body and mind knew Puerto Rico might not be the place I was karmically or dharmically designed to inhabit. It felt like, since leaving Costa Rica, my nervous system had become dysregulated again.

Of course, I could have just returned to the mainland U.S., but that didn't feel like much of an option. I had just packed all of my earthly belongings and moved my whole life to Puerto Rico, and my desire was to stay for at least a year or two before continuing on my journey to another location. I tried to speak more Spanish, learn the rhythm of how things operated there, and feel the specific energy in their culture. Unfortunately, I had to do all of that while many locals looked at me with disdain, sometimes hatred. I could see it in their eyes and feel it in their unspoken energy. Sometimes, it was even spoken out loud.

There are stark differences between living in the mainland U.S. and a U.S. territory. I don't think we, as U.S. citizens, know enough about what goes on in the outlying territories that our country has taken it upon itself to conquer and subsequently try to govern. What outsiders have done to Puerto Rico has caused animosity and a pain that runs deep. To some Puerto Ricans, if you look like those responsible for that pain, you're treated as such.

Thankfully, I also met very warm, inviting people, the opposite of those who left me confused or in tears. Once I was able to explain who I was and why I was there, and to do so in rough but distinct Spanish, many people relaxed and said, "Oh, you're not one of them." But this was something I sure didn't have a handle on those first few months. I was merely trying to stay alive, employed, and fed, and that was infinitely harder there than in the center of Tucson, Arizona.

Even after preparing and planning ahead as much as possible, life was very challenging in Puerto Rico. Living on Caye Caulker bore certain similarities when it came to dangers and logistical issues. The tiny island operated on five generators and a small water plant, but with only 2,000 inhabitants and a few square miles of land, Caye Caulker was relatively stable. Coupled with the fact that we were also only a forty-five-minute water taxi ride to the mainland from there and a thirty-minute ride to another inhabited island, civilization was never too far off.

In Puerto Rico, though, it wasn't pretty when we lost power or water—and sometimes both. The island didn't operate on public generators; if we lost power and you didn't have your own backup source, you didn't have electricity. If you didn't have gallons of water or a water cistern on your property when electricity shut off, you didn't have water either. Over time, I learned that my preference every single time was to have continuous power and be left hunting for water, rather than the other way around. (So far, at least. Note to revisit this when thirsty.)

Along with adapting to a new island, environment, culture, and an instant demand for more Spanish language skills than I possessed, my first two months in Puerto Rico were spent living in a tiny, 150-square-foot apartment full of mold. When I moved in, the bathroom faucet was barely dripping (and still was when I moved out), and I discovered mold behind the mirror above the sink. Then, once the autumn rains started in a deluge toward the end of week two, I discovered the whole apartment wept rainwater. Rain ran down the walls and the only window, to pool under the door and onto the floor. I had to brace much of the floor with rolled-up towels to keep the leaking water from invading the middle of the living space or getting my office equipment wet. Tired of practically having to use an umbrella indoors, it was time to look for a new apartment.

Luckily, my second apartment was zen, comfortable, and decorated in calming ocean blues and grays. No matter what chaos was happening around me, it became my safe haven. With all of the newness coming in from all different directions, I was grateful to have one aspect sorted out.

In some ways, it seemed as though any direction I turned, I was being blasted with water shooting out of a firehose. Returning to a somewhat big-girl job—business hours, Monday through Friday—wasn't something I had wanted, but I had prepared for it. I had to continue getting proficient at the new job while working toward my end goal: to continue traveling and writing and be abundantly compensated to continue doing so. Once that happened, I would retire to a tiny jungle bungalow with a gorgeous, enlightened man who is completely captivated by my magic and attitude—my "mag-itude," if you will—and a boy cat who secretly likes only me and treats the second human in the house as his personal butler (if I have to choose one or the other, I'd be deliriously content with just the cat. Sorry, fellas).

Besides the basic goals of being abundant in health, finances, and love, I also wanted to finish writing a book, become functionally fluent in Spanish, and allow the island to teach me what it offered. Then, I had planned to move along in my journey to encounter all the other people, creatures, and places I needed to discover. The plan sounded similar to my time in Belize and Costa Rica, each of which had taught me vastly different things. I had come so far, learned so much, and dealt with plenty of adversity, yet I kept coming back for more lessons.

I didn't want to struggle to function so much in my everyday life—here or anywhere, for that matter. Being "strugs to func" just adds an extra layer of difficulty to the daily agenda that I didn't want to deal with anymore. I felt like an ice skater with a pretty outfit but pantyhose that would only pull up to my knees, tripping me at every attempted flip or turn.

Every time I left the house or made a local phone call, I was either told my Spanish was fantastic or I wasn't even responded to because I sounded different or used the wrong words and verb conjugations. Several people asked if I was from Spain or Brazil. My tongue was butchering Spanish in a way that made people think I was multilingual, affected less by my Mexican-influenced studies and more by the Caribbean dialects I'd been recently exposed to. I'm not sure why the responses were so inconsistent, but I felt either like an overly praised, pretty little pageant child or a hairless, toothless Gollum, being wordlessly stared at as if I'd invented a new dictionary no one approved of.

I don't feel we truly understand another culture until we know something, whether verbal or non-verbal, about their language. As Heidegger said, "Language is the house of being." For each group of beings, it is how we make meaning, a shared understanding of how our immediate world works. In the Caribbean especially, Spanish is influenced by the various groups of people that ended up there, whether indigenous or migrated, coerced or forced.

Puerto Rico actually turned out to be a beautiful and interesting island full of adventure and a lot of complicated history. Perhaps I had a little too much adventure while trying to get settled and establish residency there, but nothing good comes easy. At times, it felt like I was on the cast of *The Hangover* (Parts 1, 2, *and* 3)—without the alcohol (sadly) and violence (thankfully) but not without the absurdity, disbelief, and need for quick thinking. This displaced little pixie-sized cougar managed to roll all five main characters' ridiculous experiences into one. And there wasn't even much point in trying to enjoy a cocktail from time to time because I got long COVID and could barely taste or smell anything except dill pickles, canned corn, and hot sauce. Oh, joy.

I knew that no one was coming to rescue me; certain things I would have to do on my own. As I learned the ropes of my new home in Puerto Rico, I wanted to find a way to make a positive impact on my community, which is such an important part of feeling settled in. Even though I had left Belize in a hurry, I knew I had made a positive impact on the people I had come into contact with. The few I had been able to say goodbye to had told me. I wondered how I could make a positive impact in this new place, too, with the gifts that I possessed.

My mission in Costa Rica had been more about self-salvation than trying to help others. Especially for women, when we feel exhausted and generally discontent with some facet of our lives, we have to put on our own oxygen masks before assisting others—just like they tell you to do in an airplane. You can't pour from an empty cup; you must pour into yourself first. In Costa Rica, I had gotten to a place where my cup was full and my nervous system was properly regulated again.

Even though that had started to slip once again, I was able to bounce back more quickly than I had before. I stayed active, walking to take care of my errands or visit the beaches, finding yoga and dance classes, and eventually joining a gym to regain some physical strength. With a fuller cup, my goal in Puerto Rico became one of advocacy. It was important for me not to be one of "them" (stereotypical gringos) while not being an asshole (a general aspiration of mine, not just while inhabiting Puerto Rico). My mission was to prove that there were some outsiders who loved the island and were respectful of its beauty and the people, while acknowledging its struggle. I might not have had the resources to be a significant part of the solution, but I was absolutely not going to be part of the problem. I hadn't flown in with a big bag of money to buy up land or businesses, and I wasn't going to increase the already insanely high costs of real estate, food, and other resources. I merely wanted to be comfortable in my own skin and blend in with the community on the island I now called home. I wanted to feel like one of *them*.

And then it finally happened. It felt like the island and its inhabitants were starting to see me as one of their own—at least on certain days. I was getting a feel for where I was going, whether walking or taking the bus, and I didn't have to look at maps or stress about directions. Occasionally, people even responded to me in Spanish instead of giving me a judgmental look before responding in English. I'd gotten so used to fighting hard to feel like I belonged there that I almost had an existential crisis when I noticed actual progress was being made.

One day at a restaurant, halfway through my meal, I switched to English while speaking with the waiter. Laughing, he tilted his head back and said, "I thought you were Boricua!" It made my day to be referred to as the term Puerto Ricans call themselves. Though I don't want to be anyone but myself, and I will never be Boricua, I still didn't want to stick out as much as an outsider.

Another time, when a man overheard me speaking to a waitress, he asked from his table if I was speaking Portuguese. I laughed and repeated what I had said, sheepishly explaining that I often got that feedback from people. The man smiled and told me he was Peruvian, not a local either, adding that I might get that reaction because my Spanish sounded a bit like singing. I didn't fully know what it meant that my words sounded musical, but it sure felt like a compliment, and when I was able to have relatively successful Spanish conversations, it did make my heart sing. After that, I considered Spanish my siren song—in the alluring and appealing sense, not the dangerous sense.

Being abroad had taught me so much already, and living in Puerto Rico was no exception. Resilience was again at the top of the list, but there were added layers this time. Establishing myself, working a full-time job, and finding medical and dental care were things I never had to trouble myself with the year prior. Aside from one urgent care visit (with an American doctor in Belize) and an eyeglass replacement after the ocean swallowed mine (with an English-speaking eye doctor in Costa Rica), I hadn't needed medical care abroad until living in Puerto Rico.

When I needed more advanced care, it was up to me and my limited Spanish. Whether I needed blood drawn, an X-ray, or a mammogram, I had to walk into a hospital or lab and find a way to express myself. I don't know what I had expected, but I did my best to not get frustrated and to communicate my needs. I didn't always succeed. I learned the life I'd chosen for myself—the extraordinary, anti-normal path less chosen—was always going to have more challenges. I knew it would still be worth it, though; I moved forward in life now with that belief.

Needing a short break from the big city, I rented a car and toured around the island for a week, encountering all kinds of memorable creatures, human and otherwise. Most memorable was Memo, a Boricua man I met on the fourth day of my trip once I had made my way from the north to the east coast to the south coast and finally to the west, where he served as the host of a sweet rental property. The property had a guest suite, which I rented for the night, hoping to head into the mountains the next day.

Memo and his land animal, a dog named Cruz, were a striking pair. Cruz was friendly, sweet, and, like his guardian, reserved. For twenty-four hours (which turned into forty-eight) I lived in the guest suite at the back of this huge house the two occupied. At first, I was a bit worried to see that all of the doors between my suite and theirs opened, leery of being unexpectedly walked in on after a recent episode, two days prior. (Without knocking, a hotel attendant burst into my room to answer a question I'd asked him—and, after my reaction, I'd be surprised if he ever opened a door on a guest again!). Memo may very well have been some sort of serial killer pervert, but he was so affectionate with Cruz and even dressed him in a bright turquoise swim shirt before he took us to the beach, so I just couldn't be afraid of him. Yes, he was also incredibly good-looking, so I may have been partially mesmerized by that. In any case, if the Universe wanted me to get murdered by this disheveled, oddly sexy, dog daddy surfer dude, so be it.

Memo was a born and bred surfer, bodyboarder, and

all-around tropical island guy. He was one with the ocean and all of its moods, and he kept those qualities close to the surface. He was also the perfect host because he grew up four miles away and was passionate when he spoke about his native home. I could feel his pain as he spoke about certain things that had been done to him and his island. Not many people know of the heinous treatment, human experiments, and horrific conditions forced onto Memo's ancestors at different points in history, both distant and recent. In spite of the land's turbulent history and several attempts to live on the mainland, Puerto Rico had always called him back.

Memo was a curious creature, like one I hadn't seen in a while. He was happy to serve, show, and tell, and always with a uniquely safe energy. I noticed this after speaking to him for a while, the first day I arrived. His kind eyes held the darkness and light we all have, but it all seemed to be at the surface with him. Though he seemed practiced at keeping both balanced, he constantly seemed to be struggling with more darkness than light. It was like his heart was shallow water: safe and transparent but with an overwhelming potential to grow inexplicably murky very quickly. On several occasions, I witnessed him practicing meditation and got the impression he was a very "handle with care" type of person.

When I woke up on the second morning of my stay, I knew Memo would be gone because he'd told me it was his birthday and that he would be going to get breakfast and then visit the ocean. He didn't go into the ocean much anymore, he had explained—and it was true, even when he turned me and Cruz loose on Borinquen Beach, Memo only sat under a palm tree and meditated. He had been born of the sea, and I wondered what had happened that kept him out of the water now. When I asked if he had any birthday plans with friends later, he said he didn't really celebrate his birthdays with big events.

When he returned later that day, I wished him a happy birthday, and we hugged, just because. When we did, the entire world melted away. He had a way of holding so tightly; it was so grounding, and I had absolutely no designs on leaving that embrace. We held that hug longer than was dictated by societal norms, and it was so good. Finally, as our chests touched, he said, "Heart to heart," with a smile in his beautifully accented voice. I replied that since hearts lean slightly towards the left, we needed to switch directions. He laughed, and we adjusted and continued hugging. Touching this unique creature was a surreally wholesome and safe experience beyond what I typically got from men. In fact, I wouldn't hesitate to throw a few "fish" from my collection back into the sea if I could get another hug from Memo.

When I wondered or wished or hoped that I might see Memo again, I thought of another guy in my life. And I took it as no coincidence that this shoeless, shirtless, board shorts-wearing man's name ended with the syllable "Mo." When I thought about it, Memo and Mo seemed oddly similar. Sure, one was human and one feline, but they were both a little wild, coming and going whenever they pleased. They both made me feel incredibly special and lucky when they chose to spend time with me.

Though Mo was free to roam the jungle twenty-four hours a day, most days he chose to stay with me, even between meals, as I sat and wrote or napped in a hammock. The best relationship I've had in a long time was when I fell in love with that talkative little stray cat. Mo wouldn't let anyone else near him, but he let me pet him, pick him up (once in a while), and nap on the bed together. He was the very best companion, right when I needed it the most.

Memo didn't have to take me to the farmers' market, the beach, or to the live music playing down the street. He certainly didn't have to jump in his truck to retrieve a cup of coffee for me like he did one morning or make tea for me the next day when I started to feel sick. He chose to. I felt lucky and incredibly blessed to feel the energy and love from both of my half-wild Mo creatures. This special name had been in front of me the whole time.

I had finally reached a stage in life where I had vowed to learn from all of my recent experiences of loving and letting go, whether they were decisions of my own volition or someone else's, with human or non-human creatures. I came to realize that in many of my relationships, imbalances had occurred when one or both of us had been tamed too much. In other words, love me but leave me wild. This was a beautiful opportunity for me to care for a creature but leave him wild, as I also wanted for myself.

Moving forward with this philosophy, when I started to develop feelings for a man, I paused to take a few moments—and sometimes even days or weeks—to remind myself that I needed to let us both be wild. If I felt tempted to "tame" another being, whether it was a full-grown lion or one of my beloved cubs, it wouldn't be fair or honest to either of us.

I wanted to love fully and love hard, which, to me, ultimately meant loving one man at a time. This might seem contradictory to my stance on wild-ness, but it's not like I was intending to take on a whole football team—or, in keeping with my favorite metaphor, an entire pride—at once. That's not what I meant by being wild. To me, the notion meant loving and honoring each other without taming each other's spirits. I'd seen how the alternative went in relationships such as my marriage or even my short time with Rasta, and I didn't want to go back to either scenario again.

In truth, I knew it might be hard to find the kind of romantic relationship I really wanted and deserved. So be it. Until some incredibly lucky motherfucker walks up to me and says the words I need to hear, I may just be cruising the beach and buying expensive cans of tuna to share with a few cats. I'm good with that life, unless I hear those magic words: "I promise to keep you wild."

"'RIEN NE VA ARRÊTER MA QUÊTE
POUR TE TROUVER.' NO ONE
WILL STOP MY QUEST TO
FIND YOU."

– Susane Colasanti

chapter thirteen

THE SNAKE AND THE SOAP

Even living in a foreign, tropical place again, my "ansias de conocer el mundo" (wanderlust) hadn't gone away. I wanted to discover other nearby countries and islands, so I planned some solo adventures to exotic places nearby. In January, I took myself on a four-day birthday trip to Saint Croix, in the U.S. Virgin Islands. Once there, I "kidnapped" a hotel security guard who took me to dance to some bachata music, and then I got "kidnapped" by a sexy local, who took me on an early morning hike to the beach. I had a blast.

Two months later, I found cheap flights and a hotel and went to the Dominican Republic. After getting oriented to my room and touring the exquisite art on the walls of the hotel, the receptionist informed me I could wander anywhere to the right of the building but nowhere to the left. Noted: I was not in the mood to be kidnapped (at least not *that* kind of kidnapped) on my first solo trip to the D.R. So, I explored the streets of Zona Colonial, my new favorite neighborhood (to be honest, it was the only neighborhood I'd been to in Santo Domingo, so I was admittedly biased). What followed were plenty of *Eat, Pray, Love*-esque moments inspired by the island (and an island man—same difference).

I had been a little apprehensive about visiting the Dominican Republic, which some protective loved ones had warned me about, but some sightseeing helped calm my nerves. I started familiarizing myself with the neighborhood that would be mine for the next four days, focusing on regrounding and finding balance, which is always important for me after flying. Right away, I noticed that the architecture of Santo Domingo was spectacular (and the men were so good looking)—ay dios mío! Soon enough, I was walking through a busy tourist area, with bustling historic courtyards, restaurants, and music buskers.

While making sure to remain vigilant, I was coaxed into a small store by the hottest man, selling cigars. At first, I only saw his back as I walked right past him. I don't smoke, so I had no reason to visit a cigar shop, but I knew he was yelling for me to turn around. Even just walking by, I could tell he was very handsome. He had a beautiful tone to his voice, and (don't judge me) I wanted to see his face.

I turned around to get the full view of a very good-looking face and glimpsed directly into his sparkly, shiny eyes. They just glittered, matching a killer smile with unnervingly perfect teeth. He sure was in the right line of work: he could get anyone, including non-smokers, to buy cigars. And, with such a sweetly seductive smile and those mesmerizing eyes, I could only imagine how many tourists he'd conned out of their clothes. I didn't even want to think about his global body count.

I spent thirty minutes in the shop with Jon, speaking only Spanish so he assumed it was the language we were going with. When I finally slipped into English, not able to go further in Spanish, he giggled and exclaimed that I'd had him fooled. Usually, he could tell where people were from, and with me he had guessed Spain. Laughing and talking, I watched a cigar being made and even tried to smoke a tiny one. I got him to do some bachata dancing, which he said he had been wanting to learn, and then I left. But before I did, he put his phone number into my phone and told me to call him if I was going to go out that night.

The next day, I turned the same direction out of my hotel doors (to the right, *not* the left) for more exploring and came across Jon again. His cigar shop was on the same street as my hotel and much of the tourist area was past it, so I had to walk through that area to stay in the safer, more scenic parts of Zona Colonial. As we sat outside the shop and talked, he smiled big and confessed that I had "captured him" with my eyes.

That afternoon, I met a group of bachata dancers and instructors who were starting a ten-day retreat. They were all so friendly and disappointed that I wasn't continuing with them on their travels. I was way out of my league because I didn't know how to dance traditional bachata like I did the more modern, slower style. But there were some salsa and merengue songs, and I could hold my own for those. Well, I could try.

There are certain activities and situations in my life that expose my wild nature, subtly or not so subtly. Partner dancing is outwardly observed from bystanders, but the real energy exchange is between the two people on the dance floor. Somehow, in spite of my fairly strong-willed, independent nature, I had no trouble being led around a dance floor by a variety of men. First of all, that could be because I love the music: bachata, salsa, merengue, cumbia, reggaeton, kizomba. Second, as with anything, it boiled down to energy and connection. With the right connection, I enjoyed being a "follow," the dance position traditionally taken by females. A "lead," then, is typically the man in a dance duo—but I've had some stellar female leads, both professional and non-professional dancers.

How did a wild cat like me allow myself to be led around a dance floor, manhandled into positions and turns and sexy body rolls? Well, finding a dance lead in a man who was confident and smooth but didn't suffer from an ego complex is a rare occurrence. It lets me feel the music, connect briefly with another human, and feel safe enough to relinquish control. Something happens internally that allows me to find calm even while dancing to fast, rhythmic Latin or African music. Certain muscles and joints remain alert and ready, but my body as a whole could finally relax.

The truth was, I was exhausted from being me, always on guard and looking out for danger. So often, off the dance floor, I was the one "covering my six," which required an overabundance of masculine energy. On the dance floor, I was able to let go, let the lead do what he does, and just listen to the music as my body flows with the movement cues. I'm fairly certain I could say the same about sex (Note to self: conduct some research!).

A partner dance can take on so much dimension and energy that you really feel it deep down inside. It has the power to energize and revive your spirit, helping you through a rough day (or week). That's what it does for me, anyway. But if the dance is bad or doesn't feel right, like if I feel uncomfortable energy from my partner, the experience could actually leave me with negative feelings. I'd rather have only a couple great dances in a night and leave on a high than dance with a bunch of random people, not knowing what I'm in for.

Over the next few days in the Dominican Republic, I spent quite a bit of time at the shop with Jon, and on one of my three nights there, we met for a drink. I noticed that outside of his workspace, Jon was much quieter, but we had lots of interesting conversations in Spanish and English. He was Haitian but had been living in the D.R. for seven years and seamlessly switched between his three (four, including Haitian Creole) languages. Like Rasta had, Jon asked about my zodiac sign. I learned he was a Pisces and born in too recent a year—but, hey, at least he was old enough to rent a car!

We left the bar and walked the streets of Zona Colonial, enjoying the perfect weather and sipping from Corona beer bottles. I could feel how fun and spontaneous Jon was. He had a joyful energy that showed his appreciation for the good in life. I knew he must have seen some less than joyful things in his short thirty-four years, which made his way of embracing each moment that much more inspiring. As we walked along, talking and laughing, I let him playfully spit fountains of his beer into my mouth. I'm not sure if I was really buzzed or just caught up in the moment, but we both found it completely hilarious. For someone who usually has her situation situated—a real "umbrella in case it rains" kind of girl—I didn't even mind the beer trickling down my face. I was having fun and felt completely safe.

I had already been dancing that night with the bachata group, but I wanted to do a little more, and we came upon a cute bar near my hotel and ducked in to look around. Inside, we ran into some of those new friends, and I introduced Jon to one of the dance instructors since he had mentioned that he wanted to learn how to dance bachata. We stepped near the dance floor both facing that direction, and stood still for two seconds before his arm quickly snapped around me, sucking me backward up against him. I gasped and emitted a surprised laugh, but I felt wary of this man letting his machismo loose and possibly trying to "mark his territory." I wanted to dance with anyone I chose and didn't want other guys not to approach me because of Jon and this seemingly possessive statement.

When I voiced my concern, he explained that that was how his culture shows care and protection of a partner. When he said that, I realized that my usual fight-or-flight tendencies weren't activated with this stranger. Something about him allowed me to set aside my exhausting state of alarm and relax into safety. So, I was a little perturbed, but that quickly subsided. I was happy standing this way with him.

That night, he walked me to my hotel and asked to come inside. I suspected it wasn't because he wanted to read the Bible that was tucked into the nightstand, so I explained that I wouldn't have sex with him after knowing him for only two days. I also explained what being a "cougar" meant in Western culture (since I didn't know the Spanish word equivalent for "an older woman who dates younger men"). He did his best to respect my preferences, and I did my best to only let him put one of my boobs in his mouth the next day in the back of the cigar shop. He told me he loved my petite frame, blue eyes, and white skin and that my boob ("teta") was the perfect size for his mouth. Quite frankly, none of that was a lie.

Three nights after I left Santo Domingo, Jon and I were on a video call talking about his favorite subject: love. He admitted that he tended to fall in love very easily, and when he did, it was very deep. I knew he wasn't lying because just days after we met, he had told me he loved me. After my experience with Rasta, though, I was hesitant to take any major emotional leaps with Jon.

I noticed myself trying to find as many red flags as possible—inconsistencies, suspicious word choices, sentences that sounded like straight-up lies, mentions of money or green cards or marriage, anything at all that just seemed "off." I was already hesitant, thinking about the potential cultural differences that could break a relationship—or worse, put me in physical danger again. Not to mention, he was thirty-four and I was forty-nine.

Jon and I had an undeniable connection, but I'd learned by then that a connection wasn't enough to make a relationship work—even love wasn't. He also explained that he tended to leave quickly before getting hurt. This was how he operated to protect his heart, and he'd been through the process many times before. I didn't understand; if you're already in love with someone and they change or do something to hurt you, doesn't it still hurt even if you leave?

During one of our late-night video calls, he described what he thought I was looking for. Jon said, "You want someone who can give you peace and protection, someone who cares for you and doesn't expect anything." It seemed that he was inviting me—trying to convince me, even—to be in an actual relationship with him. But what, pray tell, was his definition of a relationship? He seemed to be describing unconditional love from a perspective I could relate to. I wanted to feel safe as much as I wanted to be free. He understood that about me and tried to illustrate the point in his own way, saying that if someone holds on too tight, I quickly slither away like a snake, or, similarly, when too much pressure is applied to wet soap, it flies out of your hands.

But how would we do this from two different countries? How would I stay wild enough to continue being content and at peace within myself? How would I keep him wild enough to make it work but not so wild that I was anxious about not knowing what he was up to all the time? Thinking about these things, I tried to hold back tears. I realized I was actually afraid to try any kind of relationship with anyone at this point, and I didn't want to tell Jon about what I was feeling. Another hot, Caribbean island man? Oy. While Jon and Rasta were both from countries in the same part of the world, their personalities and approaches to life seemed like polar opposites. Rasta had been quiet and introverted, resistant to going anywhere or doing anything. Jon was expressive, insightful, caring, thoughtful, and so good with words. He was extroverted, fabulous with people, and energized by life. He wanted to see the world, and he had big dreams and aspirations for making that happen. Even though the two men were so different, I couldn't get over the circumstantial elements that weren't so different. Everything seemed to be happening so fast, and I was terrified.

My relationship with Rasta wasn't the only one that had left me mentally and emotionally shaken. I had also been left heartbroken and disheveled by the relationships I had jumped into too quickly back in my own country, which had left me so burnt out that I wanted to flee to another place. With those men, there had at least been a shared cultural understanding between us, although one of them was also from the Caribbean. (Maybe I should treat the Caribbean like the Bermuda Triangle of dating: no fly zone!)

We can't pick and choose who we love, but it is easier with someone who's lived in the same country as me. At the same time, I firmly believed that life would be so boring if we didn't dare to embrace love outside of our cultural and national borders. I didn't want to exist solely in my home country. Why wouldn't I want to explore love with interesting, amazing, gorgeous men in international locations?

All I could do was stare at Jon through the screen. He was also quiet, staring back at me. When I finally found my voice again, I asked why he wasn't speaking. He said he didn't need to say anything because our eyes were talking (one of the best lines I'd ever heard). I could feel my heart pounding in my chest and could even see my ulnar artery pulsing as I held my phone (no, that doesn't happen often, and, yes, I know where the ulnar artery is). It felt like he could see who I was. I was exposed, and as uncomfortable as that thought made me, it felt calming in some ways. I was still very guarded, but I was convinced he wasn't a danger. It felt like Jon saw me and who I really was.

With all of these visceral thoughts and emotions inside of me, I felt like a wild animal. I remembered what I saw in all of the feral cats I loved, including Mo. A cat is never born tame; it is always wild. While our eyes were "talking" and my pulse was racing, I imagined those wild cats I had tried to tame in my childhood barn. Their eyes would narrow as they hissed, crouching and searching for escape. Their heartbeats and breathing sped up, just like mine. They didn't know if they could trust me, just like I didn't actually know if I could trust Jon. Someone was trying to touch them, and they were backed into a corner. All they felt was danger. But, finally—after hours, days, or even weeks—their whole body relaxed. They got comfortable in my company. The taming had begun.

As Jon and I held eye contact over our phone screens, my facial expression, heart, and breathing softened. It was the "kitten tamer" effect. He told me more than once that it was important to him to protect the hearts of those he loved, especially when commitment, compromise, or sacrifice was involved. He was only able to make a little progress with me then, maybe because I didn't currently feel like he was trying to conquer me, but I knew that was ultimately what he wanted. Men conquer; they pursue. We even talked about that, and he admitted that was how men operated. "They conquer," I said, "and then they leave."

I don't remember his reply, but he acknowledged me for who

I was: someone who loved her freedom and was trying hard to avoid being conquered, just like those wild, little barn kittens of mine. Granted, I rarely saw a cat, once domesticated, who would have preferred to be turned loose in the snow to eat out of an old boot after living in a safe, comfortable house where two meals materialized each day. But did they know at the beginning whether it would be dangerous or advantageous for them to accept my love? Or was that something they couldn't know until I tamed them?

I finally said, "I'm scared," to which he replied, "Love is scary. But don't be scared. Don't question it; just let it be. I got you." He told me my outer self was doubting my inner self, which knew I was capable of anything. If I just trusted in that, I would be an inspiration and have a great impact on others. He added that that kind of impact would be far-reaching, well up until my eighties. (That would put him around sixty-five.)

When we got off the phone, he texted, "Don't question anything, baby. You already know everything. Just take me like a white paper and write your own story."

Because I'm a skeptical Capricorn, I responded, "How many pretty tourists have you said this to?"

"You're the first one," Jon replied. "We have a lot to learn together, not because we don't already know them, but in another, different way. I understand your language. I'm in your world."

Well, all of a sudden it seemed I was in a relationship with the youngest oracle on the planet. I could tell he had seen far more than your average thirty-four-year-old. He was old and very young at the same time, with sparkly eyes that looked playful unless he was delivering some of his trademark knowledge. Then, they became darker and deeper, making it impossible to look away. Just like he claimed I had captured him with my eyes the moment he saw them, he had captured me the same way.

We talked every day for two to three hours, covering a lot of topics—especially love (well, love and sex. Can you blame us?). Jon had a beautiful, handsome face. His smile started with his gorgeous mouth but involved his whole face, including those eyes that were so active and dreamy. Judging by his wisdom around life and love (women, specifically), he'd either gained a whole lot of real world experience or had read enough books and watched enough porn to be some sort of unofficial sex and relationship expert. And don't even get me started on how sexy his voice was. Oh my god. No matter which of his four languages he was speaking, all of his words come out sultry as fuck. It should honestly be illegal to be as hot as he was.

In certain moments, the Universe had me feeling mad, sad, and definitely confused. Why would she do this to me? Why introduce another lovely, hot character into my timeline? I would not (she tried to say convincingly) follow my heart to a foreign country so soon after meeting a gorgeous stranger. It was too "on brand" for me. It was probably time to stop calling these men "characters" and start calling them "lessons." And I was so damn grateful this lesson had fallen into my lap because knowing Jon taught me an extraordinary amount about life, love, and feeling safe. Though I couldn't explain why, I felt emotionally, mentally, and physically safe with him, even talking from a distance.

But the distance didn't last long. After talking daily for eight weeks, I booked another ticket to the Dominican Republic. This time, we wasted no time getting into bed together. After days and nights of sex, talking, and occasionally napping, we lay wrapped in each other's arms, and he asked about my previous relationships. Jon was naturally inquisitive and loved to talk about anything and everything. He wasn't afraid to ask questions or describe past relationships and even sexual encounters. He was emotionally intelligent in a way not many other men have been. It was refreshing—almost too refreshing—to see what an open book he was.

When he asked if my ex-husband was black, I said no but that everyone since him had been. Jon wanted to know why that was, and I said I thought it might have started with a specific someone. He continued to press me for the story. Then, against my better judgment, I began to tell him about the ghost that still haunted me, the lover that started it all. Wow, that was an emotional story I'd had no intention of telling, especially while naked in bed with another lover. As I told the story of James, Jon just held me tighter.

As our week together progressed, the cultural differences between us became really noticeable. How could they not? In a romantic relationship with someone who was born and raised in a vastly different country, there's bound to be a steep learning curve and extra challenges to overcome. I heavily used U.S. English slang terms and swear words that Jon wasn't used to. (It made me realize just how often we rely on the word "shit" in place of nouns, verbs, *and* adjectives!) And I wasn't used to someone taking such care to ensure I'd eaten or had a nap. Jon cared for me when I was feeling run-down and told me which vegetables, fruits, or medicinal herbs I should mix together to ingest. He was almost like an insanely sexy babysitter I never knew I needed in middle age and a sex god who was also some kind of witch doctor.

As I packed my belongings to leave Jon and the Dominican Republic one more time, my heart broke a little. Jon made me feel dirty and clean at the same time—mysterious, captivating, and somehow innocent. With him, I felt cherished, protected, and seen. His magical energy was magnetic and powerful, and I felt it every time I saw him. Being lucky enough to be near him, to be held and kissed by him, was something I'd never forget. And the sex was on a level that transcended everything I'd experienced since James. With both of them, it was a mental, emotional, physical, sexual, and spiritual practice that seemed to involve the gods, ghosts, and spirits of ancient times. Who knew what the spirits were doing while we were getting busy? Most likely watching in awe because that's what I would have been doing, had I not been an active participant. Have you ever had sex so good that you think the two of you invented it? Holy shit.

I think what was scariest of all was that Jon did sort of tame me. Just a little. And I didn't resist; it was voluntary and involuntary at the same time. But what wasn't voluntary was my will to keep some of the wild and all of the freedom I'd gained in the last two years—that part wasn't negotiable. What Jon started to tame was a different part of me: my heart.

When it really came down to it, my story started and ended with James and Jon. The rest of these "characters" were necessary experiences, all of whom taught me lessons, provided excruciating truths, and fulfilled soul contracts. But these two were the bookends, the ones who took hold of my heart in a way that wouldn't let go. My reunion with James sent me down the path of love and discovery that led me to Jon.

Some lovers leave behind something indescribable that lingers in the heart. No matter what would come of this unique and potentially very fleeting relationship, one thing was apparent: I would never be the same, and I would be better because of it. Regardless of its longevity and its unlikely and unconventional start (again), I would forever be grateful to this foreign man I had met on vacation in a foreign country (again).

There's no way to show appreciation for a gift as important as what Jon gave me, but on that trip I tried to. I showed him with my love and my body, thanking him in as many ways as I could, and after that week, I was left aching, physically and emotionally. My body and heart hurt, but only out of love and gratitude. Jon taught me more about myself and about love than anyone else I'd ever encountered up to that point. I loved him, and I always would. I was sad to leave, but we both needed to return to our own worlds. I was forever changed by that week, and who knew what the future might look like?

I knew Jon was going to do great things and go to great places, with or without me. He will always be the one who never got away because it was not my intention to capture him or make him feel trapped. I had captured him with my eyes, and he had tamed me in some necessary ways, but we were never meant to capture each other permanently. We had held on to our relationship for almost six months, but I knew I had to let go. Neither of us wanted to, but it was for the best.

Three island boys, three Caribbean islands, three different countries. As I headed back to Puerto Rico, I decided I was on a "three strikes you're out" policy on island men. I needed a little break because the coincidences were too much to deal with. So, I was implementing a temporary pause on boyfriend applications (at least if you hail from an island). Sorry for the inconvenience; please check back in the future, and thank you for your patience.

Looking out the window over the vast, blue ocean, I reflected on the past few years and realized I had truly come to understand what it feels like to belong everywhere and nowhere at once. I no longer belonged where I had originally come from, and that was okay. I realized I wasn't a tree. I wasn't rooted down, and I could go wherever I chose. My life challenged the notion that our roots are defined by where we began. In reality, they are defined by where we choose to belong.

"THERE IS PEACEFUL. THERE IS WILD. I AM BOTH AT THE SAME TIME."

— Nayyirah Waheed

chapter fourteen

THE WILD WAS ME

The crowing roosters down the street from my apartment at 4 a.m. had been replaced by a noisy jackhammer and circular saw at 8 a.m. I looked out the window to see the same construction crew that had been there for the last four months. Four months of those mind-numbing sounds. Across the street, an iguana crawled across a large branch and jumped, jostling dry leaves as it landed beneath the mango tree. One of the tame stray cats my landlords fed crossed in front of a car, giving zero fucks as to its speed.

I had seen and heard that same cacophony of sounds many days while living in Costa Rica too, but something about this was different. My life was different. I was still dealing with the growing pains and discomfort of learning how to adjust to another new way of life.

Then, I chose to lean into it—all of it. Because I was and still am under the impression that to grow and expand our hearts and minds, we have to test them, put them to work. How do you advance in school training? You are tested. It's how we learn certain fundamentals. But the rest, the rest you have to learn by doing, going out into the world and having experiences. There's no other way. Your other option is to stay where you're at, stay in one place, stay comfortable: red pill versus blue pill theory. In the 1999 movie *The Matrix*, taking the red pill means waking up to a painful truth about reality, while taking the blue pill means remaining in a comfortable, simulated reality, making the choice to stay in blissful ignorance.

In life, there are different forms of discomfort. There's the discomfort of knowing deep down that you're not where you should be or doing what you should. That type of discomfort feels like settling, possibly for a life you aren't even sure how you arrived at, and wondering "what if?"

This is different from being uncomfortable because we are experiencing growth, expansion, or evolution. That second type of discomfort comes after the initial realization and subsequent efforts—small or gigantic—to change something. For some, that can look like being more intentional with where your energy goes, with who or what you spend time on, or with healing parts of yourself, physical or emotional.

We don't always feel we have the tools or resources to enable us to choose a life that fills us with joy and purpose. It took bravery and courage to reach a new level of understanding, both of myself and of the few parts of the world I'd seen. I could have settled for the status quo, but I knew I was destined for more. To connect to my wild self, I had to be brazen and bold and fearless. Luckily, the only way I knew how to do something was to be afraid but to do it anyway. I had stayed at that first level of discomfort for the better part of forty-seven years. When I hit that second level, I went big, for better or worse. I suspected that looking for "more" would be worth it, and it was.

In Costa Rica, I experienced the closest I'd ever come to a

joyfully ecstatic daily existence. With just me, a few new friends, and my exceedingly cherished half-wild, half-domestic cat, Mo, I was enveloped in strong, maternal, healing energy. There were a few random romantic "entanglements" but no main man, no epic love, and no wild, sexy stories—though there were plenty of sexy men in that part of the world. Ladies, do yourselves a favor and take a trip to the southern Caribbean coast. Surfers, artists, dark-skinned Rastafarians, gorgeous faces and bodies that make it impossible to look away ... eye candy for days!

There, I was able to "not be so hype." Amid that overwhelming feminine energy, nothing felt forced (even my schedule, which didn't exist). I was able to slow down, reflect, and gain perspective on what I needed and wanted to change in my life. I could breathe and think about what I wanted the rest of my life to look like, insofar as I had a say in it. Growth was nurtured through me, through the soil and the sand underneath my feet.

Since leaving Costa Rica, I can still feel that feminine energy when I'm safe and grounded or standing beside someone who is capable of taking care of me. I'm grateful to have had a handful of these experiences, even after returning to Puerto Rico from the Dominican Republic. I recall the mantra I created almost ten years ago: "I lead with my heart; my heart stays open." It has been directed toward plenty of beautiful humans, many of whom had king potential, worthy mates for the Cougar Queen. I have found some truly magical and amazing qualities in them and learned some very valuable lessons along the way. Lessons about compromise. Lessons around communication, verbal and physical. Lessons about different definitions of love and sacrifice. Lessons about passion, seemingly strong enough to burn down buildings or obliterate planets. Another lesson—now, this is a novel concept—could I have been part of the problem? Gasp. That just couldn't be (she said sarcastically).

As much as my story was influenced by my heart mantra, it was never a directive toward humans only. I've had the honor of caring for many creatures during my time on this earth—the adopted dogs, the barn cats, the cat I kidnapped from outdoors to make into a house hobbit, and even my outside farm animals— each of whom brought out the maternal, feminine energy in me. My desire to mother and care for them was so intense, I often gave more of myself to that pursuit, more than most people would have. It's the closest I can come to understanding the sacrifice and love a mother has for her human child. I won't change a diaper or wipe a human nose, but I've lain in a kennel to comfort my dog (or, more likely, to comfort myself) as he recovered from surgery. I've also lain in a pile of hay at three o'clock in the morning in very chilly weather so that I could assist one of my goats in giving birth. Many sleepless nights, I've worried about my animals.

My heart feels incomplete if I'm not in close proximity to a cat for at least a few hours each day. Even though they're judgy little assholes who shit in a box for you to clean up after, they are mystical beings sent from a higher plane. But as much as I've adored all of my domesticated house pets, "tame" by human standards, I was never happier than when it was just me and Mo.

Mo has been one of the most cherished creatures in my life, and the relationship we had was perfectly balanced coexistence. Mo may have only cared that I was the person who fed him, but I became more of who I am by his side. We both could come and go as we pleased, and we did because we chose to stay wild. Neither one of us was overly demanding of the other (unless he wanted a third or fourth meal), and I directed a little mothering toward him, which allowed me to do the same toward myself. I worried about him a little, but I had faith he would find his way home. And if he was ever unable to, I knew how lucky I had been to share the time with him I already had. I strive to find that same sentiment in new relationships and experiences, especially romantic ones.

While I don't want my man patrolling the jungle at night like Mo did (or the concrete sidewalks, for that matter), I need to feel some wildness from him while also feeling content and safe. I want to sit next to my partner and feel some of those "Mo cat" qualities that balance my masculine and feminine. I want the feeling of contentment, of my heart feeling "home," while also recognizing that the individual next to me is partly wild, full of magic and endless capabilities, and predictably unpredictable— not like Rasta was; like I am.

My king needs to possess his own goals for adventure, self-improvement, and story, without stifling my ability to love or discover the wonder in this world. Where's the emotionally intelligent guy who acknowledges that I'm a highly sensitive badass who clearly needs a big hug and a forehead kiss, followed by some hot passion and light choking (yes, it's consensual!)? Then, we might hop a flight to an island for the weekend, simply because we can. Just like Mo, I'm tame but also wild.

But what now? How do I stay wild, untamed, safe, stable, true to myself, and soft in my feminine energy? To accomplish so much of what I had over the last several years, my masculine energy had taken over, and there has to be balance. I had experienced that balance before, when what emanated from the natural world and the people in Costa Rica rectified my masculine and feminine energies. Now, I wondered where I wanted my place in the world to be, what that looked and felt like, and if anyone would accompany me.

Existing in this new discomfort and "fighting" to find my own way have been excruciating at times, and certain decisions have been difficult for those who love me to witness or understand. But they were my choice. I chose which level of discomfort I was willing to experience. I chose not to be an observer inside the proverbial monkey cage and, instead, to *literally* sit down with monkeys in Panama, observing them for hours on end as I reflected on myself and my life. I chose to open my cage and get out in the wild, just like I knew I needed to be.

And I love that person I've become. She needed to be born. That's kind of how growth works: we step away or out of ourselves for a moment in order to grasp the gift of knowledge we were meant to take away. But, remember: no one is coming to rescue you. No one will be able to tell or show you the intended way a particular lesson is meant to manifest for you. It's up to you to have the experiences, the loves, the heartbreaks, the ups, and the downs, and then to integrate them into your own being, taking from them what you need. The rest of us are just witnesses.

We act, or react, and then we process the lessons we experience. Being in love is a lesson too. It offers some immediate validation of our feelings, of whether we enjoy feeling a certain way. Then, when the aftermath hits—when we feel the heartbreak and time passes—we are offered the perspective to absorb and process what it meant for and to us. Hopefully, good or bad, there's a lesson about what we do and don't want to repeat. And hopefully, we recognize it and follow its guidance. Alas, if this described normal human behavior, this book would no doubt be a hundred pages shorter.

Despite all of the crazy, funny, scary moments, I found more peace (and I found it inside myself!). Well, shit. That sounds so fucking cheesy, doesn't it? But it's true. I will never return to who I was before, now that I'm always carrying these experiences and lessons forward. I am a badass woman who has learned to trust the inner masculine while realizing the inner feminine needs to be cherished and developed so that she, too, can flourish. I've been forever changed by this journey, though it took a lot of untraining. My nature was not nurtured. But now, I know what I like, and I know what I want. I know who I want, and right now, it's me. I want me.

To live as the main character is a brave beginning—but even stars are shaped by the constellations around them. We must choose ourselves first—become the beating heart of our own unfolding—but still, it is often the presence of others that shapes who we are meant to be. "We're all just walking each other home." When we enable and support the new lessons and evolutions that occur in those around us, we allow for space and expansion in ourselves. That's how we all become better, wiser, happier—all of the things.

I may have to continue travelling frequently to different inspiring places and cultures, toward different humans, breath-taking loves, to experience all of the best parts of life. So far, they're just not in one place. That sentiment to me feels too much like I'm chasing something, but I don't feel like I'm chasing anything, actually. Because like any wild cat, they rest. When they get restless, they roam. When they're hungry (horny), they hunt. They return home, and rest again. Such is the life of a cougar.

acknowledgments

The only constant in my journey has been the desire to write my own story, while welcoming the threads of others to interweave with mine. Thank you for coming along on this journey with me, a journey that isn't finished yet.

Huge thank you to Dr. Max, who once told me—and thousands of his students—"Own your story, or it owns you." It's a truth that has echoed through every chapter of my life. For sixteen years, Max has been a constant: first, as my professor, then, my employer; and, always, my friend. He's witnessed every season—every shift, every leap, every heartbreak and homecoming. With sage advice, fatherly care, and a library of true stories that always seemed to arrive right on time, Max has guided me with wisdom and warmth. He was my *Tuesdays With Morrie*, the kind of mentor who shows up, stays present, and never lets you forget your worth, combined with a TED Talk, a campfire story, and a perfectly timed dad joke. (He also grills a perfect steak!) A prolific author himself, he never let me forget that I had something to say—and that the world needed to hear it. His belief in me has been a steady light, and I am endlessly grateful.

To my two best girls: Mandy (OG) and Seneca—my ride or dies—who listened to every early draft, no matter how rough. Your open hearts, wide eyes, and genuine excitement for my words gave me the courage to keep going. The way you lit up at each new paragraph meant more than you'll ever know. You are my biggest cheerleaders and the altruistic epitome of women supporting women.

To my editorial and publishing team at Awaken Village Press: your thoughtfulness and countless hours helping turn this part of my journey into a book have been incredibly meaningful to me, and to you I give thanks. And to Amanda, my book doula: I wrote the words, but you gave me the encouragement to speak them. Thank you for holding space for this story and for me through every rewrite, doubt, and late-night stretch.

To my mom, who now calls me Jungle Girl: her endless curiosity (and equally endless questions) are a testament to her deep care, concern, and unconditional love. Our bravery has taken different forms, and though she hasn't always understood mine, she's never stopped loving me or being proud. For that, I'm profoundly grateful.

For my brother who left too soon—Joey: I wish you could have been here to see this. I carry you with me, always—and I think I did you proud.

For friends and acquaintances, old and new, or those I met along the way while this story was being lived: thank you for your genuine excitement and interest in wanting to hear this story when it arrived fully into the world. Well, it's finally here.

about the author

Kimberly Anne is a writer and vivid storyteller who believes in following a path with heart. After years of searching for purpose in all the "right" places but feeling they were a little wrong, she discovered that the truest answers came when she took her biggest leap to discover other cultures and corners of our world. Her first book offers insight into the start of the journey and discovery of following your heart, searching for the not-so-obvious path you were meant to take. Kimberly Anne invites her readers to do just that.

When she's not writing, you'll find Kim walking along the beach, strolling down any road to talk to all of the stray cats, clumsily practicing Spanish with anyone who's patient, or dancing salsa or bachata to Latin music. She currently lives in the Caribbean.

www.ingramcontent.com/pod-product-compliance
Lightning Source LLC
Chambersburg PA
CBHW020237130626
46549CB00005B/1939